INERTI GUIDANCE

C000097976

by

CHARLES S. DRAPER

PROFESSOR OF AERONAUTICS AND ASTRONAUTICS
HEAD OF THE DEPARTMENT
DIRECTOR OF THE INSTRUMENTATION LABORATORY

WALTER WRIGLEY

PROFESSOR OF INSTRUMENTATION AND ASTRONAUTICS
EDUCATIONAL DIRECTOR OF THE INSTRUMENTATION LABORATORY

JOHN HOVORKA

LECTURER IN AERONAUTICS AND ASTRONAUTICS
STAFF PHYSICIST AT THE INSTRUMENTATION LABORATORY

MASSACHUSETTS INSTITUTE OF TECHNOLOGY

A Pergamon Press Book

THE MACMILLAN COMPANY

NEW YORK

1960

Distributed in the Western Hemisphere by
THE MACMILLAN COMPANY · NEW YORK
pursuant to a special agreement with
PERGAMON PRESS LIMITED
Oxford, England

PRINTED IN GREAT BRITAIN BY THE ALDEN PRESS, OXFORD

CONTENTS

CHAPTER 1

THE BACKGROUND OF
INERTIAL GUIDANCE

Introduction

Guidance is the art of controlling the path of a vehicle so that some desired result is accomplished. For example, a passenger airplane is guided from take-off at one airport to a landing at its destination, or a ship is guided from one harbor to another. Similarly, a missile is guided from its launcher to the vicinity of the preselected target, which may be a moving vehicle or may be stationary on the earth.

The guidance systems of manned ships and aircraft are usually made up of special instruments monitored by human navigators.[1,2] For obvious reasons, automatic guidance equipment is required to direct the movements of missiles and other unmanned vehicles. The details of guidance devices for manned and unmanned vehicles vary greatly in detail, but the functions to be performed are basically similar in all cases. The general nature of these functions is illustrated by Fig. 1-1 in terms of a radar guided missile that is intercepting an aircraft target. The physical situations and the devices that are needed to achieve guidance are suggested by the pictorial diagrams and by the elementary functional diagram, which indicates working relationships among the components involved.

The *vehicle control system* shown in Fig. 1-1 performs the two following functions:

1. It adjusts the instantaneous orientation of the missile so that it maintains stable motion substantially along a *flight reference direction* established by the mechanism of the control equipment.
2. It receives *correction command signals* and adjusts the *flight reference direction* so that the *actual missile velocity* approaches the *desired missile velocity*, which generates a path leading toward collision with the target.

The *guidance system* of Fig. 1-1, on the other hand, receives radar data on the actual position and actual motion of the missile with respect to the target, compares this information with information stored in the computer on the desired position and desired motion, and generates a *correction command signal* suitable for properly changing the flight reference direction. This correction command signal is the essential input for the vehicle control system, which makes corresponding system adjustments in the flight reference direction and then stabilizes the motion of the missile along the corrected direction. This process of guiding the missile continues to establish and maintain the desired path of collision with the target.

The pictorial and functional diagrams of Fig. 1-1 represent in general terms the components that combine to provide guidance for a vehicle. The essential outputs of the overall system are the direction and motion of the vehicle itself. The missile control surfaces adjust these geometrical quantities by applying forces to the missile structure when driven by actuators. The actuators are operated by input-power variations that are determined by actuator power controls that change the flow of energy from a power supply in accordance with *missile orientation correction* signals from the *correction command and orientation deviation receiver.*

This receiver usually includes gyroscopic units that provide signals representing angular deviations from a reference direction that is determined by adjustable settings of the gyro-unit mechanisms. When the actual orientation of the missile varies from this reference direction, orientation correction signals are generated by the receiver and supplied to the actuator power controls so that the missile control actuators force the missile control surfaces to produce a turn toward the reference direction. The correction command and orientation deviation receiver also receives correction command signals from the guidance system and shifts the reference direction so that the missile is moved toward the desired path.

In general, a guidance system has the three following functions:
1. To establish the characteristics of the desired path.
2. To receive physical inputs to establish the actual positions and motion of the vehicle as these quantities determine the actual path.
3. To generate correction command signals that will serve as inputs properly to change the reference direction existing in the vehicle control system.

Establishing the characteristics of the desired path can be accomplished

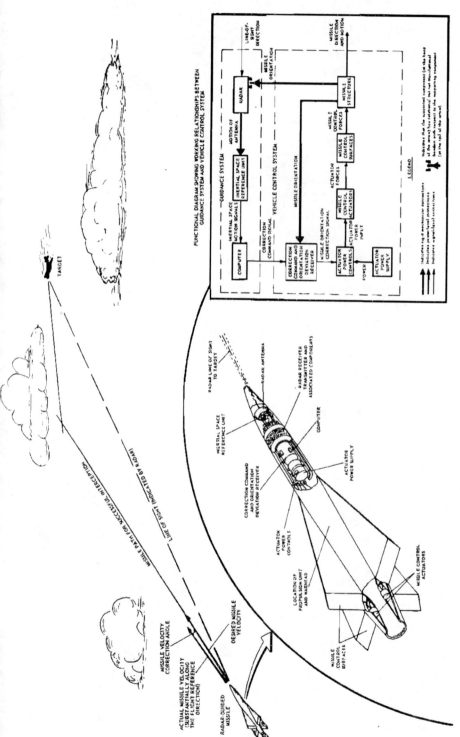

Fig. 1-1. Diagram illustrating basic concepts associated with guidance.

either by basic design of components or by means of memory units incorporated in the equipment. For determining essential information on actual vehicle paths, various principles are available for use by guidance systems. The means shown in Fig. 1-1 for purposes of illustration is an active radar carried by the missile structure, with rotational freedom for tracking the line of sight to the target. Angular velocity of the line of sight with respect to inertial space is represented by signals from gyro units mounted rigidly on the antenna structure. With these signals as inputs, the computer (which contains data on the desired course) generates correction command signals representing the flight-direction changes to be carried out by the vehicle control system.

Vehicle control systems must be so intimately associated with vehicle structure and operation that they are normally considered as part of the vehicle itself. The design, manufacture, and application of vehicle control systems are well-established arts and may be treated as matters of routine. Guidance systems, on the other hand, are currently just entering the stage of large-scale production, and their problems are far from having reached the point of generally accepted standard solutions.

This book is primarily concerned with the theoretical and practical problems of guidance systems, and especially with the principles of inertial equipment that promise high levels of performance in ships, submarines, aircraft, and missiles. The book includes a description of the means used to realize inertial guidance, a review of the available history of the art, an exposition of various system types, a treatment of essential components and their design features, and a discussion of the current state of production and applications of inertial guidance systems.

Elements of the guidance problem

Movement in the direction of desired goals has been a common activity ever since members of the human race first inhabited the earth and learned such skills as propelling hollowed-out logs across the water toward home or hunting ground. Each trip of this kind involved guidance in the sense that the man involved had to have a destination in sight and had to change his direction as required to move toward his goal. The geometrical elements involved were very simple in that turns were made toward one side or the other of the man himself in order to correct any movement away from the direct line of sight. In effect, the only geometrical idea required was that of direction with respect to the man involved. The guidance problem became somewhat more complex when the line of sight to the destination was obscured by a hill, a forest, weather, or distance. Here, the geometry involved needed to be extended to include visible landmarks different from the goal, but having known locations on the earth with respect to the goal. By using a sufficient number of intermediate guidance points fixed to the earth, it was possible to use terrestrial coordinates for guiding overland journeys of any length.

Terrestrial coordinates are not sufficient for guidance purposes over large areas of land without visible known landmarks, and the difficulties are multiplied for voyages that are over water and out of sight of land. Long ago, men found that problems of this kind could be solved by using properly selected celestial bodies as guidance landmarks. Experience with this procedure over hundreds of years has produced the refined celestial navigation that is in common use today. Rotation of the earth on its axis and revolution about the sun require chronometers and almanacs as essential elements in celestial navigation, but from the standpoint of basic geometry this method depends on the use of the celestial sphere determined by the fixed stars as an auxiliary guidance space.

Inertial guidance is based on geometrical concepts that are essentially similar to those of celestial navigation, with the space determined by the fixed stars replaced by an inertial-reference space associated with a rigid member that is an integral part of the guidance equipment. The orientation of this member is held unchanging with respect to the fixed stars by means of an arrangement including gyro units, gimbals, and servomechanisms. This *inertial-reference unit* provides a set of reference coordinates that is directly available for guidance purposes and offers the great advantage of functioning without any external contacts made by means of light or any other form of radiation.

Basic geometry of guidance systems

Figures 1-2, 1-3, 1-4 and 1-5 illustrate the geometrical concepts that are suggested in the preceding section. The diagrams of Fig. 1-2 show situations wherein the destination is directly visible and radiation contacts, either optical or by longer-wave radiation, give information on deviations from direct-approach paths. These deviations naturally appear in coordinates fixed in the guided entity, whether it be a man or a machine.

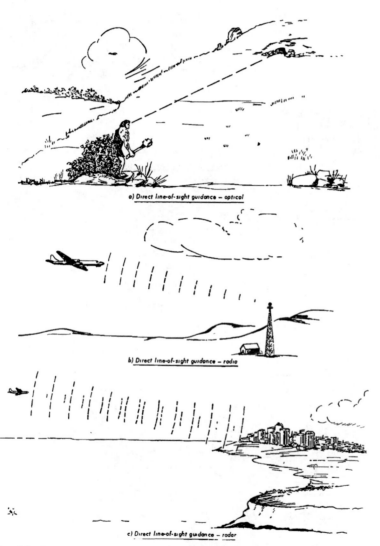

a) Direct line-of-sight guidance – optical

b) Direct line-of-sight guidance – radio

c) Direct line-of-sight guidance – radar

Fig. 1-2. Direct-line-of-sight guidance; only coordinates fixed to guided entity are required.

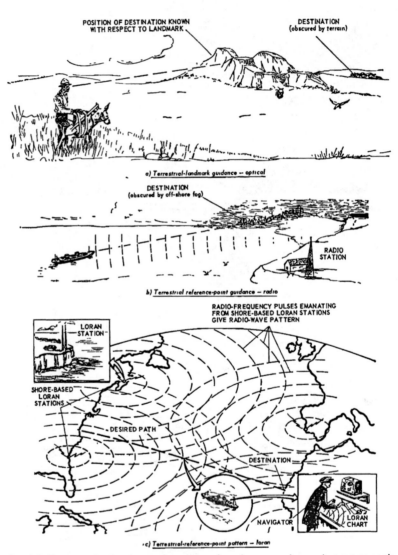

Fig. I-3. Terrestrial-reference guidance; use of earth space to locate destination with respect to accessible reference points.

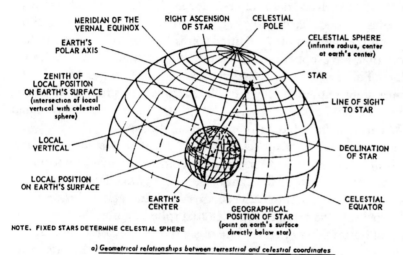

a) Geometrical relationships between terrestrial and celestial coordinates

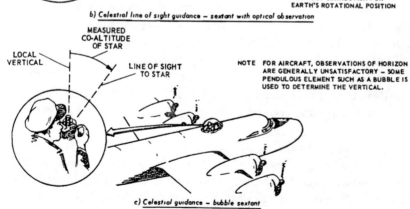

Fig. 1-4. Celestial reference guidance—use of celestial space to provide auxiliary reference points for finding terrestrial positions.

Figure 1-3 illustrates the class of situations in which a direct line-of-sight contact with the destination is not available. This makes it necessary to use a space fixed to the earth for auxiliary reference coordinates in which the position of the destination is known with respect to landmarks that have optical or other radiation contacts with the guided entity. This *terrestrial-reference guidance* in its simplest application requires information on only a few landmarks; in its most sophisticated form, with radio and radar networks, it must depend on accurate maps of the earth, with radiating points carefully located.

Figure 1-4 suggests the essentials of celestial-reference guidance, which may be used when terrestrial-reference guidance is not possible because natural or artificial landmarks are not available. Figure 1-4a illustrates the relationship between terrestrial and celestial coordinates, with fixed stars determining the celestial sphere. Figure 1-4b shows the essential observation of a star line of sight and the horizon made by a human observer using a sextant. Figure 1-4c represents the same situation, except that a bubble is used as a pendulous device for indicating the vertical. In all navigational observations, the essential measured quantity is the angle between the direction of the local vertical (the direction in which a simple pendulum would hang when suspended from a base fixed to the earth) and the line of sight to a selected known star.

Situations exist in modern guidance practice in which terrestrial or celestial landmarks are either unreliable or not available, and when at the same time it is not desirable or is actually impossible for the guided vehicle to emit radiation, since radiation may be subject to jamming or may provide information for military enemies. For example, submarines carrying out unrestricted operations below the surface are effectively shut off from all guidance contacts that depend on radiation of any kind; aircraft flying at low levels in bad weather over unfriendly terrain are also handicapped as far as the use of radiation for guidance is concerned.

The guidance systems for ballistic missiles must be self-contained if simultaneous firing of several missiles is to be carried out with less than one radiation-operated ground control system per missile. Aside from the instances where external radiation contacts are not possible, there are many cases where self-contained guidance equipment can be very useful. Equipment of this kind is made feasible by inertial-reference units that, in effect, establish and hold a rigid member within the system to an orientation that is accurately fixed with respect to the celestial sphere. These artificially established internal auxiliary coordinates may be designed to provide all the geometrical information that can be derived from the celestial sphere. Figure 1-5 illustrates such a reference member stabilized and held in a desired orientation by a combination of gyro units, servodrives, and gimbals. A unit of this kind serves as an

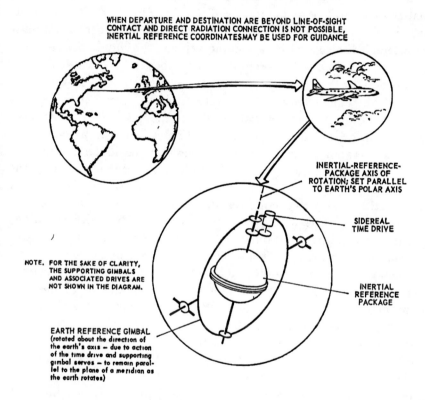

Fig. I-5. Inertial guidance—use of stabilized inertial reference coordinates for finding terrestrial positions.

inertial-space reference member. By placing the axis of support of this inertial-reference member parallel to the earth's axis of rotation, it is possible to use a sidereal time drive to rotate the reference-member gimbal at earth's rate with respect to an earth reference gimbal, so that this latter gimbal effectively holds a fixed orientation with respect to the earth as the earth rotates about its axis.

In all applications of celestial space or inertial space as auxiliary geometrical references for fixing positions on the earth, the direction of the local vertical is the physical quantity uniquely associated with an individual point on the earth. At any given point, this direction is fixed as the vector resultant of the gravitational field and centrifugal force due to the earth's rotation. When a base stationary with respect to the earth is available for use in making observations, it is a simple matter to accurately determine the direction of local gravity by means of a simple pendulum. When the base from which the pendulum must be suspended is carried by a moving vehicle, the simple pendulum is no longer adequate for accurate indications of the vertical. The inaccuracies are due to the basic fact of physics described by Einstein's principle of equivalence, which states that the mass of any given particle is the same for inertial-reaction responses to linear accelera-tion as it is for responses to gravitational fields. This means that small linear acceleration components at right angles to the direction of gravity produce changes in the pendulum angle that correspond to very great changes in position on the earth's surface. Physically the effect occurs because the total force acting on any body is the summation of the individual *specific forces* acting on each particle of the body. By definition, specific force is the resultant of gravitational force and the inertia-reaction force for each unit mass. The specific force due to acceleration is a vector equal in magnitude and opposite in direction to the accelera-tion vector. Use of this fact simplifies the combination of inertial-reaction effects with gravitation effects, because an awkward change of sign on the acceleration is eliminated.

Inertial guidance with respect to the earth is possible for vehicles moving under conditions that allow gravitational effects to be used for guidance-system input purposes. The problem is basically that of achieving accurate indications of the vertical by means of equipment carried in a vehicle that moves on a surface that is substantially spherical about the center of the earth. Schuler clearly stated this problem in the early 1920s and described a solution based on a proper selection of dynamics for the indicating system. The dynamical requirements near the earth's surface involve tuning the pendulum system to an undamped period of about 84 minutes. Systems with these characteristics are said to have *Schuler tuning,* in recognition of the contributions made by Dr. Schuler.[3, 4]

Figure 1-6 is a diagram that illustrates the physical significance of

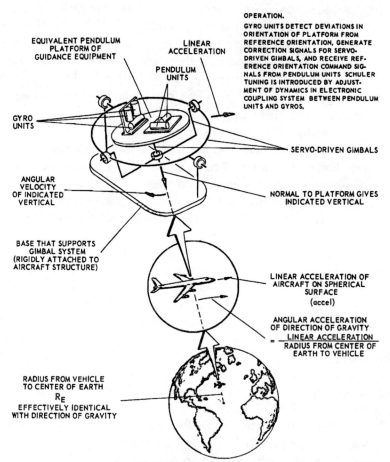

EQUIVALENT PENDULUM
PLATFORM OF
GUIDANCE EQUIPMENT

LINEAR
ACCELERATION

PENDULUM
UNITS

OPERATION.

GYRO UNITS DETECT DEVIATIONS IN
ORIENTATION OF PLATFORM FROM
REFERENCE ORIENTATION, GENERATE
CORRECTION SIGNALS FOR SERVO-
DRIVEN GIMBALS, AND RECEIVE REF-
ERENCE ORIENTATION COMMAND SIG-
NALS FROM PENDULUM UNITS SCHULER
TUNING IS INTRODUCED BY ADJUST-
MENT OF DYNAMICS IN ELECTRONIC
COUPLING SYSTEM BETWEEN PENDULUM
UNITS AND GYROS.

GYRO
UNITS

SERVO-DRIVEN GIMBALS

ANGULAR
VELOCITY
OF INDICATED
VERTICAL

NORMAL TO PLATFORM GIVES
INDICATED VERTICAL

BASE THAT SUPPORTS
GIMBAL SYSTEM
(RIGIDLY ATTACHED TO
AIRCRAFT STRUCTURE)

LINEAR ACCELERATION OF
AIRCRAFT ON SPHERICAL
SURFACE
(accel)

ANGULAR ACCELERATION
OF DIRECTION OF GRAVITY
$= \dfrac{\text{LINEAR ACCELERATION}}{\text{RADIUS FROM CENTER OF EARTH TO VEHICLE}}$

RADIUS FROM VEHICLE
TO CENTER OF EARTH
R_E
EFFECTIVELY IDENTICAL
WITH DIRECTION OF GRAVITY

NOTES 1. WHEN EQUIVALENT PENDULUM SYSTEM DYNAMICS ARE ADJUSTED SO THAT A LINEAR-ACCELERATION
INPUT CAUSES AN ANGULAR VELOCITY RESPONSE OF THE PLATFORM IN ROTATING THE INDICATED
VERTICAL, SUCH THAT THIS INDICATION REMAINS CORRECT NO MATTER WHAT HORIZONTAL LINEAR
ACCELERATIONS ARE GIVEN TO THE PLATFORM, THE EQUIVALENT PENDULUM HAS SCHULER TUNING

2 FOR PATHS NEAR THE SURFACE OF THE EARTH, AN EQUIVALENT PENDULUM SYSTEM WITH SCHULER
TUNING HAS AN UNDAMPED PERIOD OF 84 6 MINUTES

Fig 1-6 Physical significance of Schuler tuning for eliminating the effect of horizontal
acceleration on vertical indications from an equivalent pendulum carried by a vehicle
moving about the earth at constant altitude

B

Schuler tuning for the idealized case of an aircraft flying at constant altitude above the earth's surface. When this aircraft is given a horizontal acceleration, that is, an acceleration at right angles to the local gravity vector, the direction of the local vertical changes with an angular acceleration equal to the linear acceleration divided by the distance of the aircraft from the earth's center. The condition of Schuler tuning means that the pendulum system in the guidance equipment is designed and constructed so that its response to any horizontal linear acceleration is an angular acceleration about a horizontal axis at right angles to the direction of the linear acceleration and with a magnitude equal to the ratio of the linear acceleration to the radius from the center of the earth to the vehicle carrying the equivalent pendulum. When a pendulum has performance of this kind, the indicated vertical rotates with the actual direction of gravity no matter how horizontal accelerations may vary. This means that the indicated vertical holds its accuracy in a moving vehicle so that inertial guidance over the earth becomes feasible.

The mechanism of an equivalent pendulum with Schuler tuning includes gyro units to detect deviations of the platform upon which they are mounted from a reference orientation determined by the gyros themselves. Signals corresponding to these deviations serve as the command inputs for servodrives on the various axes of a gimbal system that act to maintain the orientation of the platform in substantial coincidence with the reference orientation. This action provides *geometrical stabilization*, which effectively isolates the platform from all angular movements of the vehicle in which the equivalent pendulum is carried.

The pendulums shown on the platform of Fig. 1-6 are actually responsive to specific force, which means that they swing away from the direction of gravity under the action of specific-force components due to linear acceleration. The signals resulting from the pendulum motion are the essential inputs for the electronic components that couple the pendulums to the command-receiving elements of the gyro units. Schuler tuning for the equivalent pendulum system is provided by proper design of the electronic system.

Summary

In this chapter, guidance has been discussed in terms of physical situations for the purpose of defining basic concepts and introducing the problems that must be solved by practical guidance equipment of any type. The distinction between vehicle control systems and guidance systems has been noted, together with the fact that the primary concern of the book is with systems of the latter class. The general nature of the functions that must be built into guidance systems has been described. The fundamental importance of the geometrical reference space as a factor in extending operating capabilities has been reviewed. In addition, guidance systems based on coordinates fixed in the guided vehicle, in terrestrial space, in celestial space, in inertial space, and on combinations of these spaces for geometrical reference purposes have been illustrated.

This book is essentially a discussion of inertial guidance system principles, with particular attention being given to basic theory, system organization, functional features of components, and the operating characteristics of these components. To provide a setting for this material, it is preceded—in what follows—by a review of inertial-system developments and a brief review of the gyroscopic devices that provided background technology for the inertial developments of the preceding two decades.

CHAPTER 2

BRIEF HISTORY OF INERTIAL GUIDANCE SYSTEM DEVELOPMENTS

Marine instrument developments

Orientational reference devices based on inertial principles have a history of over fifty years of use in guidance and vehicle control. In particular, the mechanical arrangement described by Foucault as the 'gyroscope'* has found wide application in geometrical references applied to instruments for navigation of the sea and of the air. Mechanically, the gyroscope consists of a rotor spinning at high speed and supported by low-friction gimbals so that its axis is free to rotate with respect to its base about an effective pivot point. The usefulness of this arrangement depends on the gyroscopic principle of precession, a special manifestation of Newton's laws of motion applied to rotation, by which the spin axis of a gyro rotor turns toward the axis of any torque applied to the inner gimbal about an axis at right angles to the spin axis. This angular velocity of precession has a magnitude that is proportional to the magnitude of the torque and is inversely proportional to the magnitude of the angular momentum of the rotor, which is the product of the moment of inertia of the rotor about the spin axis and the angular velocity of spin.

A fundamental characteristic of the gyroscope is that the angular velocity of precession is a motion with respect to *inertial space*, which in turn is effectively identical with the *celestial space* established by the fixed stars. If the effective applied torque is zero, the precession velocity is zero and the rotor spin axis holds its orientation unchanging with respect to inertial space. This means in turn that an untorqued gyro rotor holds its orientation among the stars. When the precessional torque is not zero but has a known direction and magnitude, the rotor axis changes its orientation with respect to celestial space at a rate that

---

* *Webster's New Collegiate Dictionary* gives for *gyroscope*: A wheel or disk mounted to spin rapidly about an axis, and also free to rotate about one or both of two axes perpendicular to each other and to the axis of spin.

is predictable if the angular momentum of the rotor is known and is in a direction that carries the spin axis toward the torque axis.

The marine gyroscopic compass is essentially a gyroscopic rotor combined with a special pendulum. Pendulous command torques are applied to the rotor so that the spin axis precesses in an oscillatory manner about an axis formed by the intersection of the local meridian plane and the local horizontal plane, and finally settles on north by means of suitable damping. Gyroscopic compasses[5] have been in general use for approximately fifty years and will surely continue to be basic items of equipment for ships.

World War I demonstrated the need for complete and accurate indications of terrestrial coordinates on shipboard for the purposes of gun fire control. The gyrocompass provided azimuth information, but disturbing effects due to horizontal accelerations prevented satisfactory indications of the local vertical by simple pendulous devices. This deficiency was subsequently overcome by the introduction of *stable vertical* equipment based on combinations of gyroscopic components and pendulum units. By the use of sufficiently great angular-momentum magnitudes, the effects of uncertainty torques from gimbal bearings were reduced so that the transmission of vehicle rotations to the indicating member that carried the gyro units was acceptably minimized. The pendulum unit system produced output torques suitable for commanding the gyro units to precess toward positions in which the output direction, fixed to the indicating member, was along the actual vertical within allowable tolerances.

From early in this century to the present time, many able scientists, engineers, and manufacturers have contributed to the art of marine gyrocompasses and stable verticals. The story of their efforts and achievements has been told in many references.[6] Because this material is pertinent to the present discussion only as part of the general background, it will not be reviewed in detail here.

Aircraft-instrument developments

Inertial principles are applied in marine gyrocompasses and stable verticals for the sole purpose of indicating directions, without any attempt to directly find position or velocity over the earth. Although stable verticals were in use for over a decade preceding World War II, it remained for the military necessities established by that conflict to provide the stimulus for developments to overcome the problems of blind flying by the use of gyroscopic devices. Attention was concentrated on the indication of angular quantities with respect to earth coordinates by small-size instruments, without showing motion directly. The first inertial instrument for aircraft was the *rate-of-turn indicator* based on the theory and patents of Henderson[7] in England and the work of the Sperry Gyroscope Company in America, in the nineteen twenties. The first device of this type to appear in reasonably wide use was an air-driven gyroscopic rotor carried by a single-degree-of-freedom, spring-restrained gimbal. Turns made about an axis at right angles to the spin axis and the gimbal axis caused the gimbal to tip so that the deflection of an index showed the pilot the direction and rate of turn of his airplane. Instruments almost identical with those of the twenties are in general use today.

Somewhat before 1930, Guggenheim grants for the advancement of aviation led to the first completely blind flights by James H. Doolittle and his associates. The inertial instruments that made a new era in aviation possible were developed by Elmer A. Sperry, Jr., and his associates of the Sperry Gyroscope Company. Indications of the vertical were provided by an air-spun gyro rotor supported by a two-degree-of-freedom gimbal system and precessed toward the direction of gravity by a system of pendulum-controlled air jets.[6] This instrument was originally called an *artificial horizon*, because of the nature of the indications it provided.

Aircraft azimuth indications that were free from the erratic oscillations and turning errors associated with magnetic compasses were provided by the *directional gyro*. This instrument is still standard equipment for aircraft. A directional gyro (sometimes referred to as a D.G.) consists of a gyro rotor and a two-degree-of-freedom gimbal system that supports it. A D.G. is designed to operate with the spin axis substantially horizontal to give a direction from which azimuth angles may be measured. The precessional torque required to maintain the spin axis horizontal against the rotation of the earth and vehicle motion comes from balance weights and properly directed air jets or magnetic torque units.

Gyroscopic aircraft instruments give very useful orientational indications of the vertical and of azimuth, but the performance levels are much inferior to those required for any satisfactory inertial guidance system. For example, the tolerance on angular drift uncertainties in azimuth indications is in the region of two to twelve degrees per hour.

Directional gyros have no useful capability for seeking the direction of north and, in general, can not be read to divisions that are much smaller than one degree. Similarly, bank-and-climb indicators do not give a precision better than about one degree and often exhibit 'wander' uncertainties larger than this angle. In order to improve precision and reduce wander, the gyroscopic element is generally coupled to the pendulum system so tightly that the erection rate is in the region of one to ten degrees per minute. This rate is obviously very far from the rates corresponding to the 84-minute period of Schuler tuning. This means that aircraft turns cause bank-and-climb indications having errors of such magnitudes that they may approach, and even exceed, ten degrees for a standard 180-degree aircraft turn.

Inertial-guidance performance requirements

Inertial-guidance equipment must provide performance of reasonable quality if it is to repay the effort and cost of development. The actual specifications for various systems are still not available in detail because of government security regulations concerning classified matter, but it is possible to identify broad ranges of performance that must be reached if the inertial approach to guidance is to be worthy of support. In terms of the angle between local verticals on the earth, one minute of arc corresponds to one nautical mile. It follows that if guidance inaccuracy limits are set at ten miles during a certain time period, the allowable angular inaccuracies for geometrical references and vertical indications must be less than ten minutes of arc. Assuming that vehicle speed does not affect angular accuracies, the distance travelled is not in itself important as far as system performance is concerned.

For purposes of discussion, consider a guidance inaccuracy limit of one mile during a vehicle motion lasting for one hour. If drift in the geometrical reference is allowed to absorb all of the inaccuracy, the gyroscopic units and their supporting mechanism must hold the initially set reference orientation effectively within one minute of arc per hour. Earth's rate with respect to the stars is 15 degrees per hour or 900 minutes of arc per hour, so that a rate of one minute per hour corresponds to about one milli-earth-rate unit (symbol meru). For the purposes of comparison with gyroscopic instruments for aircraft, which have drift rates not much less than one earth-rate unit (symbol eru), it can be stated that useful inertial navigation systems must have gyro drift rates at least three orders of magnitude less than those realized in conventional aircraft instruments. System design may affect the realizable performance to some extent, but the drift rate of the geometrical reference sets an absolute minimum on the accuracy that may be achieved from any practical equipment.

Specific force receivers (accelerometers) capable of working over any considerable range of inputs commonly perform with inaccuracies in the region of one per cent of maximum reading. A pendulum designed to identify position within one mile must have an angular uncertainty less than one minute of arc (about 0.291 milliradian), which corresponds to an uncertainty in acceleration measurement that is less than three thousandths of one gravity. For practical purposes, specific force receivers for inertial navigation systems should perform within inaccuracy limits at least one order of magnitude better than this limit. This means that inertial guidance has imposed the need for considerable development on specific force receivers.

Gimbal systems, servomechanisms, electronics, time drives, computers etc. for inertial systems all represented problems of considerable magnitude at the beginning of inertial-guidance work. The difficulties involved and the means used to find solutions are discussed in later chapters of this book.

Inertial-system developments

Inertial guidance as a practical art for controlling vehicle motion between points on the earth did not exist before 1940. All the impetus to start developments in this area stemmed directly from military requirements generated by World War II. Beyond doubt, credit for the realization of inertial guidance belongs to the Peenemunde group of German scientists who developed the V-2 ballistic rocket missile. Kooy and Uytenbogaart[8] note that V-2 flights occurred in July, 1942. The guidance and control system for this rocket employed two two-degree-of-freedom gyros, one to control rolling and yawing motion and the other to control pitch. The pitch gyro was also used to control the pitching over of the rocket from its initial vertical launching attitude in accordance with the precalculated desired trajectory.[9] This latter function was carried out by artificially precessing the pitch gyro by means of a pitch discriminator coil in the guidance and control system. The relative motion between gyro and gimbal was detected by a fine-wire potentiometer whose output signal, after being amplified by thyratron tubes, was transmitted to the appropriate control surface.

While early models of the V-2 used Doppler radio techniques to determine fuel-cutoff velocity, this method was soon dropped in favor of an integrating accelerometer[8,9] by means of which the rocket became independent of ground control. This accelerometer consisted of a gyroscopic pendulum mounted in a gimbal. As the pendulum deviated from its neutral position, it switched on an induction motor which rotated the gimbal so that the pendulum was caused to precess to its neutral position. By appropriate recording technique, the acquired speed of the missile was obtained.

The German group had under development at the end of World War II a stable platform using three single-degree-of-freedom gyros, employed in conjunction with an integrating accelerometer to take into account the inclination of the flight path to the vertical.

A number of German scientists and engineers under the leadership of Dr Wernher von Braun came to the United States after the end of World War II and brought with them the inertial-guidance techniques and equipment that had been developed in connection with the V-2 missile. Their work has continued, under sponsorship from the United States, and has produced successful guidance systems for several missiles, notably the Army REDSTONE and Army JUPITER rockets. Details of the equipments developed and their performance are not available because of military security requirements, but it is common knowledge that militarily valuable results are being obtained from commercially supplied equipment.

American efforts in the field of inertial guidance were all started by the Air Force after the end of World War II in the 1945–1946 period. Situations of three types were attacked that did not include those involving ballistic missiles. The problems to be solved were those of bombing from manned aircraft, delivery of warheads by subsonic winged missiles, and delivery of warheads by supersonic winged missiles. No requirement existed for ballistic-missile guidance, as this type of missile was not yet under development by the Air Force.

Three contract arrangements were destined to bear fruit in the form of complete systems carried through engineering tests. In September of 1945, the Instrumentation Laboratory of the Massachusetts Institute of Technology received a contract to design and build a stellar sighting device, a stellar computer, a three-axis stabilization device, and a time base, for use in connection with long-range bombing aircraft. Northrop Aircraft Inc., under Air Force sponsorship starting about June of 1946, began development of star trackers, gyros, computers, and apparent-vertical direction indicators with the objective of providing guidance for the SNARK high-subsonic-speed missile. The Autonetics Division of North American Aviation Corporation, with Air Force support, began development of guidance equipment for supersonic bombing missiles about April of 1946. The Hughes Aircraft Company also started guidance system work in the late forties, but soon withdrew after some initial work on components.

In the beginning, American guidance developments were not directed toward completely inertial systems, because of existing doubts that such systems could overcome the difficulties of realizing components of sufficiently high performance. For this reason, the proposed Instrumentation Laboratory system included automatic tracking of celestial bodies, and the first Northrop system was based entirely on automatic seekers for star lines of sight as a means for providing the necessary geometrical reference space. North American also applied star tracking in various systems to improve guidance performance.

As experience with design, construction, and tests of guidance systems accumulated, all of the Instrumentation Laboratory systems and several of the North American systems became completely inertial, and the complications of celestial-body tracking were eliminated. Northrop systems moved away from all-star-tracker-control and toward increasing dependence on the inertial properties of gyroscopic components. In general, the processes of stellar-inertial system development are still active, but for various reasons the flow of information on design details is slow; however, it appears that guidance systems are generally coming more and more to rely on inertial principles.

Flight tests with successful results were made with the Northrop and North American systems in 1954. No records are publicly available, but it is reasonable to suppose that the test programs have continued, since 1954, to generate information of importance for the realization of improved guidance.

Instrumentation Laboratory work on inertial guidance[10] was a direct continuation of studies in aircraft instruments started at the Massachusetts Institute of Technology in 1930. These studies were largely concerned with gyroscopic devices from the standpoint of basic theory, design, and manufacture and with applications of inertial space to the operating problems of aircraft and naval vessels. The theoretical aspects of these problems received much attention in graduate courses and research work associated with regular academic work at the Institute. World War II developments of gunsights for warships and aircraft fully occupied the capabilities of the Instrumentation Laboratory until the end of 1944. At that time, discussions with the present Major General L. I. Davis, Dr J. E. Clemens, and members of their staff at the Armament Laboratory of the Air Force's Wright Air Development Center led to the initiation of a project directed toward the development of nonradiating bombsights for Air Force planes. The great difficulties to be overcome before any project of this kind could be successful were realized. Details were necessarily vague, but the great improvements to be made in gyro units, specific force receivers, servodrives, amplifiers, time drives, etc., were recognized. With the excellent understanding and support from the Air Force, all of the essential problems were attacked at the same time, with the clear realization that several years of continuous and coordinated effort would be needed before the possibilities and limitations of inertial-guidance systems could be established. The Instrumentation Laboratory has consistently followed this plan since 1945 with support from both the Air Force and the Navy in advancing the state of the inertial guidance art by building and testing systems of various types. These types have been selected to cover the full spectrum of theoretical and practical problems associated with inertial guidance. The systems that have been built and tested, either by the Instrumentation Laboratory or by agencies working with this laboratory, are reviewed briefly in the following paragraphs.

The FEBE (a variant of Phoebus Apollo, the sun god) system was designed for the purpose of experimentally checking the basic principles of geometrical stabilization, floating integrating gyro units, high-performance specific force receivers, servodriven gimbals, electronic accessories, time drives, computers and the many other items making up a guidance system with automatic tracking of celestial bodies. The first flight tests with the FEBE system were carried out during the spring of 1949. Test runs were made between Massachusetts and New Mexico in a B-29 aircraft that required about ten hours for the one-way trip. Results did not indicate that FEBE could be considered as a production prototype, but they did show that the chances of achieving satisfactory solutions for all the problems of inertial guidance were good enough to justify further developments.

In 1948, support was provided by the United States Navy for a project to design, construct, and test a combination gyrocompass and stable vertical based on the principles demonstrated by the FEBE system. Laboratory tests of the shipboard system, which was called MAST (Marine Stable Element) were started late in 1952 and were followed by shipboard tests in 1953. The studies that had been carried out for MAST and the preliminary tests of the subsystems suggested that a complete inertial navigation system for naval vessels should be possible. This possibility was suggested to the Office of Naval Research, with the result that a study was begun in June of 1950 and submitted to ONR one year later. On the basis of this study, development of the Submarine (later Ship) Inertial Navigation System, called SINS, was started by the Instrumentation Laboratory in March, 1951.

SINS was completed in the spring of 1954 and given preliminary tests in a trucking van. Shipboard tests followed six to eight months later, and a final report was submitted in June, 1955. The results were of such quality that inertial guidance was incorporated in submarines designed to fire POLARIS missiles.

While the work on SINS was carried out for the Navy, inertial developments were continued under Air Force sponsorship. Design of the SPIRE system (abbreviation for Space Inertial Reference Equipment) was started in October, 1949. This fully inertial system was given its first transcontinental test flight in February, 1953. On the basis of the encouraging results from the SPIRE tests, a system of reduced weight and improved performance, called SPIRE, JR., was begun in July, 1953; testing of this system began in January, 1955. This system was used on an inertially guided transcontinental flight in March, 1958 that was recorded in motion pictures and used by Eric Sevareid in his April 13, 1958, 'Conquest' television program. Flight testing of the SPIRE, JR. system was completed at the end of July, 1958.

The Instrumentation Laboratory started work on inertial guidance for ballistic missiles as a subcontractor to the Convair Division of General Dynamics Corporation early in 1954. This effort was shifted to Air Force sponsorship early in 1955, after the Ballistic Missile Division under Lieutenant-General B. A. Schriever had begun operations. The resulting laboratory developments supplied the basis for the inertial-guidance equipment manufactured for the THOR missile by the AC Spark Plug Division of General Motors Corporation. This company and the International Business Machines Corporation now have the responsibility for production of inertial-guidance equipment for the TITAN ballistic missile. This development is based on a design started by the Instrumentation Laboratory in January, 1954, and tested by that laboratory during 1959.

The background of inertial-guidance work available in the Instrumentation Laboratory led the Navy to assign development and engineering test responsibility for inertial guidance systems to be used in the POLARIS missile. Work on this equipment was started in the fall of 1956. As reported in the public press, POLARIS guidance systems designed by the M.I.T. Instrumentation Laboratory have been under test for some time. These tests show that design objectives have been met.

Inertial guidance systems involve many ramifications, partly theoretical and partly practical. Work in these areas is proceeding at many places under various sponsoring agencies. Rapid progress is being made, but it is doubtful that any principles beyond those that are now thoroughly understood will arise to revolutionize the art of inertial guidance. On the other hand, there is much room for improvement and refinement of the actual equipment. It is to be expected that better performance from smaller, lighter, and less-expensive systems will result from the effort that is being expended.

The following chapters of this book are intended to describe and discuss the fundamental principles available for use in inertial-guidance components and in systems that may be built up from these components. The authors hope that their efforts will assist readers to obtain a better understanding of a relatively new and necessarily somewhat complex subject that will surely be important for future military and civil transportation systems.

CHAPTER 3

BASIC PRINCIPLES OF INERTIAL GUIDANCE

Application of inertia to navigation

Since the inertial guidance of vehicles may be regarded as a funda-mentally geometric problem, its pictorialization in terms of the actual components used is possible without recourse to mathematical develop-ment or engineering detail. Picturing the problem in this way is the objective of the present chapter.

Mechanization of inertial coordinates

To say that inertial guidance is geometric is to say that it deals with the location of points in certain coordinate systems. The problem is thus solvable by the mechanization of appropriate coordinate axes,

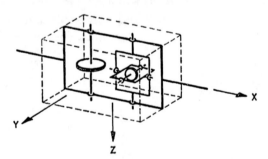

Fig. 3-1. Representation of inertial coordinates by a box containing a massive object or large gyroscopes.

that is, by the construction of physical objects which are designed to simulate Cartesian coordinate frames. It is, of course, possible to embed a set of 'body axes' in any rigid object; if it is a particularly heavy object, or, say, a box containing large operating gyroscopes, so that it is difficult to rotate, the body may be regarded as representing coordinates which do not rotate with respect to inertial space (Fig. 3-1). These coordinates—called simply inertial coordinates—will remain non-rotating with respect to their environment if they are coupled to it by a frictionless and massless gimbal system (Fig. 3-2). But inertial guidance systems actually contain models of inertial-coordinate axes which use neither heavy masses nor even heavy gyros, and in which gimbal friction is of secondary importance.

Mechanical decoupling of gyros from the vehicle

The importance attending gimbal friction stems from the fact that it transmits into torques on the gyros at the center not only the inter-fering torques acting on the vehicle (causing it to roll, pitch, and yaw), but also any torques applied directly to the gimbals. These torques will cause the gyros to *precess*, i.e., to rotate, and the instrumented inertial

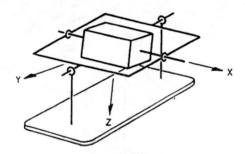

Fig. 3-2. The coupling of mechanized inertial coordinates to the environment by means of frictionless gimbals.

coordinates therefore to *drift*. Thus it will be seen that the gimbals' true function is to *decouple the gyros from the base* on which the gimbal system is mounted.

To see how this mechanical decoupling is effected in practice, con-sider that even if the gyros are not massive, their response to interfering torques which penetrate through the gimbal system to the gyros might, with suitable instrumentation, be represented by electrical signals denoting precession. These signals—one from each of the three axes—may be proportional to the rate of precession, as in a *rate* gyro. The signals may be proportional to the integral of this rate, as in a single-degree-of-freedom *integrating* gyro or a two-degree-of-freedom gyro. In the case of rate integration, the angle of precession is proportional to the angle through which interfering torques have turned the base about the gyro's input axis.

The gyro output signals are thus carriers of the information that the gyro package coordinates have been disturbed (Fig. 3-3). This information is now put to use, as shown in the figure, to overcome the bearing friction and other interfering torques on the gimbals. This requires that the bearing assemblies actually be not merely shaft supports, but involve electric motors as well, so that the gyro outputs, suitably processed, monitor the gimbal drive motors directly.

The result is thus a multiple closed-loop servo system. The gyros have the status of controllers of the inertial orientation of their own input axes, and the torque motors that of producing the desired orientation.

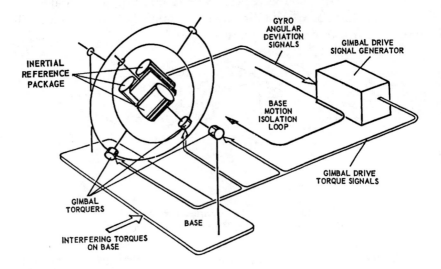

Fig. 3-3a. Base motion isolation with single-degree-of-freedom gyros as control elements and driven gimbals for decoupling the gyros from the environment.

Since the medium of control is a signal, the gyros need not be massive, and the gimbal drives furnish the rotational torques needed to stabilize this *base motion isolation* loop.

The successful mechanical decoupling of a gyro package from its environment, as shown in Fig. 3-3, does not set up any particular inertial coordinate system, however; its orientation with respect to, say, lines of sight to certain stars, or to the earth's polar axis, or to the vertical at some point on the earth, is still completely arbitrary. What has been done is to set up interference-proof nonrotating coordinates; this is *geometrical stabilization.*

Gyro command signals

There is another function which the gyro package may have: rotation in response to *command signals*. These commands are presented to the gyros individually as input currents to *torque generators* or *torquers*, which, like the *signal generators* in the gyro case, operate about the output axis— the axis of precession—of the gyro. The effect of these commands is to send signals from the gyros to the gimbal drives as shown in Fig. 3-3, which now have the function not only to mechanically decouple the gyro package from the base, but also to set the gyro package—and the instrumented coordinates—into rotation with respect to inertial space.

The base-motion-isolation loop is thus seen to provide a *torque-free-environment* for the operation of the gyros as *angular velocity command receivers*. In this connection it must be stressed that integrating gyros,

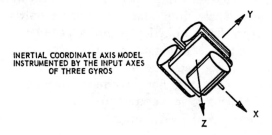

INERTIAL COORDINATE AXIS MODEL
INSTRUMENTED BY THE INPUT AXES
OF THREE GYROS

Fig 3-3b Inertial coordinates mechanized by the gyro package.

used as the representative gyro example in the figure, are null-operating devices, and that they null on the commanded angular velocity, which includes zero angular velocity in the case of inertially-nonrotating co-ordinates. The reorientation of the gyro package about some line as a result of the angular velocity command will be through an angle equal to the time integral of this angular velocity relative to inertial space. It is in this sense that the name *space integrator* is sometimes applied to a gyro-gimbal configuration of the type shown in Fig. 3-3.

Gyro drift

Internal to the gyro units themselves, a problem arises when un-expected torques cause *drift* of the wheel gimbal about the output axis. Clearly, such drift will result in false signals to the base-motion-isolation servo; and it becomes important to counteract this drift effect when it is not totally unexpected (such as when, for example, the drift can be recorded during some test period of time before the gyros are to be

c

used). *Drift correction signals* applied to the gyro torquers to overcome the drift tendency serve to maintain the status quo as far as the inertial reference of the gyro package coordinates is concerned. Such drift correction operates in addition to any angular velocity commands also applied to the gyros through their torquers. In general, drift correction signals are based on statistical averages of recorded drift, while command signals reflect the angular rates desired of the gyro.

Force measurement

In inertial guidance, inertially-referred coordinates are needed for the measurement of the total force on the vehicle. When this force is considered, it is convenient to deal with it as specific force, that is, body force per unit mass. In practice, this reduces to placing force-measuring devices in a known orientation with respect to a gyro-instrumented coordinate system. But a fairly simple force measuring system may be conceived without gyros. Even a physical pendulum can be regarded as measuring, by its angular deflection from the vertical, the horizontal force applied to its pivot to accelerate it. It will be recalled, from the discussion in the previous chapter, that a pendulum does not distinguish between gravity and kinematic acceleration in its measurement, that is, it measures specific force. A refined simulation of a pendulum can be made to draw a distinction between the force of gravity and inertia reaction force when the shape of the earth's field is given as spherically symmetric. When a system is designed to distinguish between the direction of gravity and the direction of specific force, it must have the dynamic characteristics associated with Schuler tuning.

Mechanization of terrestrial coordinates

This simulated pendulum is discussed in what follows in terms of gimbaled instruments. Gyros are omitted pro tem, since terrestrial coordinates are to be instrumented by this device, rather than inertial coordinates as in the case of gyros. The terrestrial coordinates are to be thought of as somewhat arbitrary in orientation—the x- and y-axes having any orthogonal directions in the horizontal plane, while the z-axis is along the vertical at the location of the vehicle carrying the gimbals, i.e., the z-axis is along the local gravity vector (Fig. 3-4).

It may be seen from the figure that it is similar to the base-motion-isolation setup in Fig. 3-3, except that now two specific-force receivers in a *specific-force-receiving package* replace the three gyros in the inertial reference package of the preceding figure. (*Specific force* is force per unit mass, numerically and dimensionally equivalent to acceleration.) Only two specific-force receivers are shown because, in this example, vertical accelerations can be ignored. If the specific-force receivers are to detect only horizontal acceleration components, and not gravity, the gimbal drives must remove the accelerometer package tilt, and this they will indeed do, insofar as the earth's gravity field may be regarded as spherically symmetric, provided the servo loops represented in the figure have the Schuler frequency as their undamped natural frequency. Figure 3-4

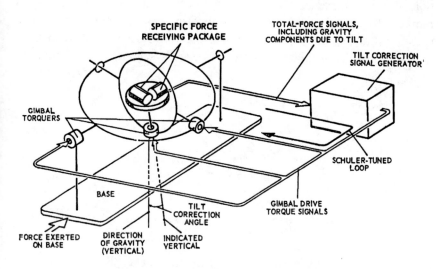

Fig. 3-4a. Vertical indication with accelerometers as control elements and driven gimbals for correcting tilt of the specific-force-receiving package with respect to gravity.

is thus a feasible vertical-indicating system for use aboard a moving vehicle.

The specific-force receivers shown in the figure are small pendulums which serve as force-measurers in the manner already suggested; the pendulum's output angle is rendered electrically by a signal generator, as in a gyro. A mass-and-spring combination will also serve as a specific-force receiver to indicate the applied specific force. For precision purposes there is a form of specific-force receiver that is more suitable than either of these. This is a gyro- and gimbal-drive combination, *single axis*, with a calibrated mass unbalance along the spin axis of the gyro, so that it is sensitive over a great range—and without saturation—to the applied force. This device directly combines for a measurement with integration and gives change of velocity as its output.

Earth-reference coordinates

A vertical indicator by itself is only one of the requisites for navigation on the earth; in addition, *earth-fixed* reference coordinates are needed, e.g., the equator as the zero of latitude, and, arbitrarily, the meridian through Greenwich as a zero of longitude. While gyros, as have been seen, mechanize inertial-reference coordinates, the mechanization of earth-reference coordinates has yet to be discussed. Finally, it remains to combine the vertical indicator and the gyros in such a manner that (1) the specific force on the vehicle is measured in inertially-referred coordinates, so that Newton's second law of motion,

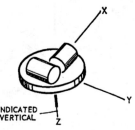

Fig. 3-4b. Terrestrial coordinate axis model instrumented by input axes of accelerometers and indicated vertical.

which applies only in inertial coordinates, may be applied to derive the acceleration of the vehicle from the force measurement, and (2) the double integral of the measured specific force, interpreted as the vehicle acceleration, giving the displacement of the vehicle, may be referred to a set of terrestrial reference coordinates, as a navigator refers his track to a course on a map.

Mechanization of earth-reference coordinates

The distinction (for terrestrial navigation purposes) between terrestrial and inertial coordinates is that terrestrial coordinates rotate with respect to inertial coordinates at the earth's daily rotational angular rate about the earth's polar axis (Fig. 3-5). To mechanize terrestrial coordinates, then, an *earth-reference gimbal* is placed around a gyro package (Fig. 3-6) in such a way that the gimbal can be rotated about a line parallel to the earth's polar axis so that it 'keeps up' with the earth, while the inertial-reference package 'stands still' inside it. The mechanism for accomplishing this is an electric time-drive motor between the earth-reference gimbal and the inertial-reference package. This is thus a

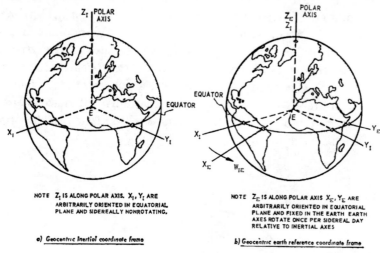

NOTE Z_I IS ALONG POLAR AXIS. X_I, Y_I ARE ARBITRARILY ORIENTED IN EQUATORIAL PLANE AND SIDEREALLY NONROTATING.

a) Geocentric Inertial coordinate frame

NOTE Z_E IS ALONG POLAR AXIS X_E, Y_E ARE ARBITRARILY ORIENTED IN EQUATORIAL PLANE AND FIXED IN THE EARTH EARTH AXES ROTATE ONCE PER SIDEREAL DAY RELATIVE TO INERTIAL AXES

b) Geocentric earth reference coordinate frame

Fig 3-5. Terrestrial and inertial reference coordinates, earth-centered.

special form of base-motion isolation, but different from that previously discussed, in that here the base motion, being due to the earth's rotation, is regular and unidirectional, so that the base-motion isolation

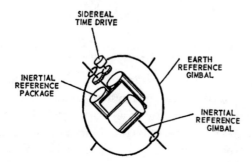

Fig. 3-6. The mechanization of terrestrial coordinates with a sidereal time drive decoupling an earth reference gimbal from an inertial reference package.

'loop' is actually open-ended. The motor which turns the earth-reference gimbal is irreversible and as nearly constant in speed as can be made: a synchronous clock motor fed by a signal from a carefully calibrated oscillator.

Coordinate origin and orientation

A certain arbitrariness in the orientation of the inertial-reference package has been removed in Fig. 3-6. One axis in the package is now parallel to the earth's polar axis; this is an *initial condition*. A second initial condition will remove the remaining orientation arbitrariness, e.g., aligning the y-axis with the normal to the meridian plane through Greenwich. The fact that the terrestrial coordinates and inertial coordinates mechanized here are not actually earth-centered, but are instead vehicle-centered, does not affect the arguments used, which are concerned entirely with *rotation* of axes. The only difference between vehicle-centered and earth-centered axes is a translation of the origin along the local earth radius (Fig. 3-7).

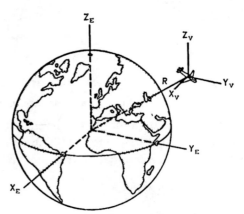

Fig. 3-7 Parallel sets of earth-centered and vehicle-centered inertial reference coordinates.

A representative guidance system: gyros in inertial coordinates

In one form of inertial guidance system used in aircraft, the earth-reference gimbal is surrounded by base-motion isolation gimbals, as well as a fixed gimbal which permits the base-motion isolation gimbal orientation with respect to the polar axis to be adjusted (the *range* isolation gimbal of Fig. 3-8). The gyros are thus mounted very much as in Fig. 3-3. The vertical indication loop is now mounted on the range isolation gimbal, which is functionally fixed to the earth-reference gimbal, as shown in Fig. 3-8. The vertical indicator gimbal drive motors thus operate in stabilized terrestrial coordinates, free of roll, pitch, and yaw—a notable operating advantage over the simple vertical indication system already discussed.

With the vertical indicated in terrestrial coordinates of known orientation, the vehicle may be located and therefore guided entirely from on-board measurement and control. During a transcontinental flight, the gimbals will be driven in such a manner as to move the inertial-reference package and the specific-force-receiving package into orientations characteristic of their functions. A series of such orientations is shown in Fig. 3-9, where the gimbals have been omitted, and the

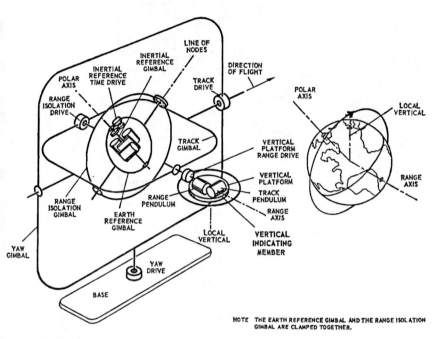

Fig. 3-8. A possible mode of coupling the mechanized terrestrial and inertial reference coordinates with force and position measurement in an inertial guidance system.

problem is presented in terms of the instrumented geometry—the mechanized inertial and terrestrial coordinates.

Gyros in geographic coordinates

In an alternative method of gimballing, the gyros and accelerometers are mounted together on instrumented geographic coordinates: local north, east and vertical. The accelerometer output signals are integrated with respect to time (and modified in less important ways) and are then used as gyro commands (Fig. 1-6). No inertial coordinates are simulated physically; instead, the initial conditions, inertially referred, are stored on integrators. Here, the indicated position change is obtained by integrating the gyro commands. Thus a system of this kind is dependent for its accuracy on the ability of the gyro commands to reflect the time derivatives of the position components of the vehicle; e.g., in geographic coordinates, these derivatives are the latitude rate and horizontal-longitude rate of the vehicle. There is a presupposition here that the inertial-reference and specific-force-receiving packages are continually

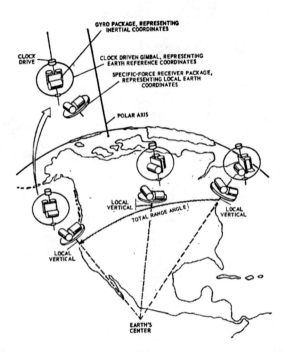

Fig. 3-9a. Successive orientations of the inertial reference, earth reference, and local great-circle coordinates on an inertially guided transcontinental flight, as seen by an observer fixed relative to the earth.

aligned with local north; this azimuth alignment may be the result of the application of a computed angular rate of the gyros and accelerometers about the vertical (the *velocity compass*) or of a north-seeking property given the system by an appropriate interconnection between the gyros and the drive about the vertical axis (*gyrocompassing*).

In any case, whatever the gimbaling arrangements, the objective is to place the accelerometers, or specific-force-receiving package, into a known orientation with respect to the gyros, or inertial-reference

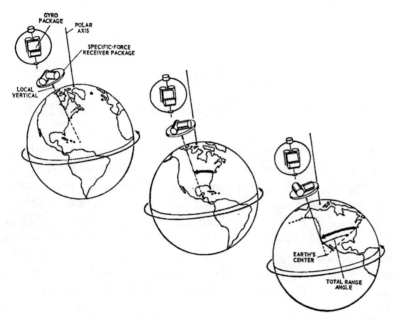

Fig. 3-9b. Successive orientations of the inertial reference, earth reference, and local great-circle coordinates on an inertially guided transcontinental flight, as seen by an observer fixed relative to inertial space.

package. Then the inertially-referred acceleration of the vehicle may be measured (making due allowance for gravitation) and the double integral of this acceleration, the vehicle displacement, may be referred to terrestrial coordinates, thus locating the vehicle for guidance purposes.

CHAPTER 4

THE ROLE OF FIELDS IN NAVIGATION

Specific-force measurement and displacement computation

The traditional procedures that have been developed for the navigation of vehicles, particularly the navigation of ships and, more recently, aircraft and missiles, are the basis for automatic position indication and automatic steering. Inertial guidance extends the techniques of traditional navigation to dynamic force measurement in a gravitational field. It is characterized in general by the making of the minimum number of measurements on the environment, and by the avoidance of radiative contact. In fact, in normal operation, only one navigational parameter is measured: the inertially-referred specific force on the vehicle. The inertial guidance system is, under these conditions, completely self-contained.

In inertial guidance the measurement of the inertially-referred force on the vehicle is interpreted by the inertial navigation system in terms of the vehicle's acceleration along its course in navigational coordinates, which is followed in turn by the double integration of this acceleration, resulting in the measured displacement along course. This displacement gives the position of the vehicle relative to some frame of reference whose orientation must be known with respect to, but need not be identical with, the reference frame or coordinate system in which the force on the vehicle is measured. This measurement and computation represent an extension of traditional dead-reckoning procedures, in which, in an analogous way, dynamic measurements on the environment are made. Thus, the integration of the output of an airspeed meter or of a pitometer log will yield a computation of the distance travelled through the medium—air or water—in which the vehicle moves. It is apparent that navigation can occur in a variety of fields, and the concept of a field therefore will be examined in some detail.

The field concept is used in physics to describe a force exerted by one body on another without their being in contact. The field is said to fill all space, and its strength at any point in space and time is measurable, in principle, by placing a test body at the point and measuring the force on the test body. Thus, a force field is the ensemble of such measurements; indeed, a force field is sometimes defined as the force on a *unit* body. In the case of an electrostatic field, the test body is a unit charge; in a magnetic field, a unit current; and in a gravitational field, a unit mass. The implied assumption is always that the test body leaves the field itself undisturbed during the measurement. The field concept may be extended to any ensemble of functions of space and time; these functions are, in general, called *field variables*. Thus, it is possible to speak of the gravitational field of the earth or the pressure-gradient field in the ocean. These are vector fields. Scalar fields which are defined only in terms of the magnitude of a quantity at some point in space and time, with no direction assigned, are conceivable as well. Examples of scalar fields are the temperature fields of the atmosphere and of the ocean and the gravitational potential field of the earth.

Navigation is based on the measurement of fields. This proposition, obvious for terrestrial navigation, applies as well to extra-terrestrial navigation. The point of view adopted in the latter case is that to leave the earth is to enter space in which force fields other than those of the earth assume importance. These latter fields are those due to the other bodies in the universe.

Navigation through static and dynamic pressure fields

The static pressure field in a fluid may be defined for present purposes as the force on a unit area of surface located in the fluid. In general, this internal pressure will be a space and time function; but, if the fluid is not in motion relative to the pressure-measuring device, it can be called the *static* pressure and is a function solely of the force field in which the fluid is placed.

Near the earth's surface, the static pressure in a fluid stationary on the earth is a function of the depth alone, if gravitational field asymmetry and the earth's daily rotation are ignored. Thus, depth measurement in the ocean and altitude measurement in the atmosphere can be effected through static pressure measurements. The applications to submarine or air navigation are obvious.

Static pressure measurement is seen to be restricted to measuring position along an axis parallel to the earth's radius, approximately. For other position data, resort must be had to dynamic pressure measurement, that is, to measuring the pressure which the thrust generator on the craft causes the craft to exert on the air or water in the direction of travel. Thus, dynamic pressure is the pressure increment above the static pressure due to motion of the craft through the medium of travel. The term dynamic pressure is usually understood to refer to a Newtonian (non-viscous) fluid, so that the dynamic pressure-speed-relationship in an actual fluid is subject to certain corrections. In marine and submarine navigation, the *pitometer log* measures dynamic pressure. The device consists of a sea-water pump which builds up a pressure head on one side of a diaphragm, while the other side of the diaphragm is exposed to the sea-water pressure increment caused by the speed of the craft through the water; under equilibrium conditions this pressure increment is proportional to the speed of the pump itself. Thus, dynamic pressure is used to measure the speed of the craft through the water.

An airspeed meter in an airplane also measures speed relative to the medium of travel; the air, in this case. An airspeed meter can take the form of a Pitot-static tube, in which the dynamic pressure is measured. The operation is simpler than that of a pitometer-log, but the quantities measured are analogous. In any case, two points concerning the use of dynamic pressure measurements in navigation should be noted:

1. The measurement as taken indicates speed of the craft with respect to the medium through which it is travelling. This will be the speed with respect to the earth only provided the medium is homogeneous and isotropic and not moving with respect to the earth. This last point calls attention to ocean currents as sources of error in using speed-logs and winds as sources of error in using airspeed meters. The fact that the pressure is approximately proportional to the *square* of the velocity means that the *direction* of the velocity vector is not determined by these devices. This is the reason for stressing the fact that speed is measured rather than velocity. Even when it can be independently determined that the course is level, measurement of the direction of the velocity requires a knowledge of at least the heading of the craft. The magnetic compass or gyrocompass must provide this datum to augment the speed measurement.

2. A second point is that the speed measurement gives only part of the desired position data. It is desired to know not merely the length of the velocity vector and its direction, but also its origin. To obtain this information from the incremental pressures actually measured requires that the system integrate the velocity of the craft; in particular, it must integrate the velocity components in some known coordinate system

(for example, the coordinate axes might be the north-line, east-line and vertical at some reference point fixed on the earth) for the craft location to be computed in this coordinate system. This time-integration of the craft velocity components measured with respect to the medium of travel is called *dead reckoning*.

It should be noted here that the temperature of the medium of travel is a scalar field, and also that temperature *gradient* (the maximum space-rate of change of temperature) is a vector field, both of which might have significance in navigation. The difficulty is one of time dependence, which not only limits prespecification, but also limits measurement, since navigation inherently converts space derivatives of field variables into time derivatives. This is true not only of temperature fields, of course; the static pressure fields and the earth's magnetic field are also noticeably time-dependent. Winds and currents are not predictable, except in a general way, in terms of specification by maps. Dead-reckoning by any method suffers from serious disadvantages.

The present status of dead-reckoning navigation

The interest in inertial navigation, which arose to supersede dead-reckoning, tended to eclipse the research and development on dead-reckoning systems. The general area still requiring exploration is the determination of the velocity of an object through a liquid or a gas, using many possible physical properties: natural properties, such as magnetic susceptibility and electrical conductivity: and induced properties, such as ionization or locally-induced radioactivity. Furthermore, the measured velocity must be integrated to get position, and drift-free integrators (digitally-operated counters) have not yet been used in this field, perhaps because of the lack of sufficiently refined sensors to back them up. Finally, the problem of automatic star-tracking enters here, in that its intermittent application could potentially augment dead-reckoning by reducing errors due to initial conditions on the integrators, as well as errors due to the time-dependence of the properties of the medium of travel, including its velocity with respect to star space.

Navigation in the earth's electrostatic field

The earth and its atmosphere support an electric field of considerable variability in space and time.[11] The field is predominantly vertical, and is conveniently specified as a potential gradient in volts per meter along the local vertical. The potential gradient is for the most part positive; that is, the earth's surface appears to be negatively charged. The gradient is about one to three volts per centimeter or 100 to 300 volts per meter at the ground level, on regular terrain in good weather. In certain regions the gradient can climb to over 500 volts per meter, particularly in rough terrain such as mountain peaks or ridges. In free air the gradient decreases with increasing altitude; for example, it falls to about 25 volts per meter at 3 km, and to 4 volts per meter at 10 km.

This potential gradient gives rise to electrical currents in the atmosphere. The atmosphere may be described by a specific resistance: over open terrain the resistance of a 'unit cube of atmosphere' between opposing faces is about 10^{16} ohm-cm; and of dry soil, 10^5 to 10^7 ohm-cm. In free air the atmospheric conductivity increases rapidly with altitude, increasing by a factor of about six in the region from 3 km altitude to 10 km altitude.

These specific resistance values are strongly space- and time-dependent. In general they do not, in the earth's potential gradient, yield large currents except in the case of lightning. The applicability of the earth's electric field to navigation is thus doubtful, unless further data (e.g., on the distribution of atmospheric radioactivity) make the field more predictable.[11]

Navigation through the earth's magnetic field

The fact that the earth has a magnetic field that can be used in marine navigation was recorded in European literature as early as A.D. 1180. This field has two poles, one in northern Canada and one in Antarctica. It is equivalent to that due to a magnetic sphere or to an imbedded magnetic dipole. The field is normal to the surface of the earth at the magnetic poles and tangent to the earth on a line defining the magnetic equator. Thus at the magnetic equator the field is everywhere parallel; and in general, the field direction is not unique. It follows that the magnetic field alone is not suitable for specifying position on the earth. *

* When an electric conductor is in motion in a magnetic field, a potential difference proportional to this velocity is induced between the ends of the conductor. The resulting current could (in principle) be used to indicate ground speed, i.e., the conductor is moved so as to cut the 'lines of force' of the earth's magnetic field. The electromotive force required to drive such a current depends on the *net* rate of change of magnetic flux through a closed circuit. Thus the present circuit would have to be of extremely large dimensions to encompass a sensibly non-homogeneous field, because in a closed electric circuit moving in an essentially homogeneous, i.e., zero space-gradient, electromagnetic field such as this, exactly as much flux enters the loop as leaves it in a given unit of time.

With the aid of auxiliary equipment to establish the horizontal plane, the magnetic field offers a valuable directional reference in this plane. This has been done for centuries with the magnetic compass. Correction for the angular difference between magnetic north and geographic north, i.e., for *declination* or *variation*, is possible because the properties of the magnetic field are quite well known for most of the surface of the earth except in the polar regions. The magnetic field properties at altitudes above the earth's surface have not been fully determined, although they are predictable through harmonic analysis.

The total *intensity* of the magnetic field is lowest at the magnetic equator and nearly double that value at the magnetic poles. The total field intensity might therefore be used to indicate magnetic latitude, but can give no information on magnetic longitude. Extensive magnetic mapping is also required before serious consideration of such magnetic navigation can be considered.

Magnetic data are interfered with by magnetic storms, which are associated with the aurora and sunspot activity. Artificial interference with magnetic data cannot be ruled out, but a large amount of power would be required to generate any effective disturbance.*

Motion of a point in a gravitational field

It will be seen from the foregoing that, while navigation has never been restricted solely to the use of the earth's gravitational field, the other fields available are subject to difficulties in interpretation in the derivation of navigation data. They suffer from non-uniqueness, both in space and time taken separately, and in the indistinguishability of space gradients and time derivatives in field measurement from a vehicle having a velocity with respect to the medium of travel.

The earth's gravitational field is far less susceptible of misinterpretation as navigation data than the fields heretofore considered. To approach the study of navigation in the earth's gravity field, the general problem of mechanics in which a mass point moves in a gravitational field will be discussed.

---

* Any physical phenomenon which relates the vehicle to its inertial-space environment is to be regarded as a potential navigation aid. Thus, cosmic rays, coming to the earth's surface as streams of particles from outer space, and whose charged component is influenced significantly by the earth's magnetic field, would constitute a navigation aid if their properties as particles, their aggregate density, or their motion could be uniquely related to position on the earth (See Reference 12)

Inertial force and field force

Newton's second law of motion, which states that the force exerted on a mass point is equal to the product of mass and acceleration, may be treated as a definition of force. (Newton himself was not clear on which was definitive, force or mass.) The force so defined expresses the inertial property of matter and is sometimes called the *inertial force*. Another property of matter is expressed by saying that two mass points attract each other with a force proportional to the product of their masses and inversely proportional to the square of the distance between them. This force can be called *gravitational force*, in contra-distinction to inertial force.

When a stationary plumb bob or pendulum is used to determine the direction of the vertical, it is (neglecting the centrifugal force due to the earth's rotation) the gravitational force that is exerted on the pendulous mass. But if the pendulum is mounted in a vehicle accelerating over the earth, an inertial force—propelling the vehicle—will be superimposed on the gravitational force. Thus, despite their apparently differing origins, the two kinds of force are not separable by direct measurement. This is an example of a more general proposition made originally by Einstein in setting up the general theory of relativity: the principle of the *equivalence* of inertial and gravitational forces. An acceleration-measuring device (an *accelerometer*) might consist of a test-mass attached to one end of a spring, with the other end of the spring attached to the vehicle whose acceleration is to be measured. The displacement of the test mass is then, according to the principle of equivalence, interpretable variously as due to an acceleration of the vehicle in a field-free space, or due to a gravitational field alone, or due to some combination of the two. As an example of such a combination, consider a vehicle that is stationary with respect to the earth. An accelerometer test mass on it then will have, in general, a displacement reading proportional to some component of *gravity*. Gravity is the vector sum of the gravitational *field* and the centrifugal *non-field* force due to the earth's (and hence the accelerometer's) daily rotation (Fig. 4-1). Summary 4-1 displays in an example the variation in the data derived from force measurements made separately by accelerated and non-accelerated observers. The 'data' are actually the measurer's interpretation of the observed displacement of a test mass. The point of view which may be best adopted here is—to return to the case of the aforementioned accelerometer—that the test mass is pulled in one direction by the spring's elastic force, and in other directions by all the other masses in the universe. The zero resultant of all of these forces, one of which is elastic, accounts for the observed displacement of the mass.

Thus inertial space is seen as a highly artificial but nevertheless convenient construct whereby acceleration can be referred to the environment, but whether this environment be interpreted as a field-free space or as a field will determine what is meant by the word 'inertial'.

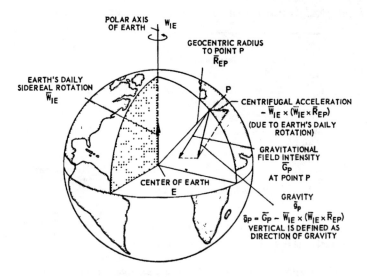

Fig. 4-1. Relationship of factors to produce the vertical.

Every body continues in its state of rest, or of uniform motion in a straight line, unless it is compelled to change that state by forces impressed on it. This is Newton's statement of the first law of motion. Since even when only two bodies are present, they do *not* move in straight lines, in general, but rather in conic sections—in hyperbolas, ellipses, or, for a body near the earth, approximately in parabolas, fields may be regarded as immaterial 'forces' which, once postulated, render this law valid. The success of navigation hinges ultimately on the predictability of the gravitational field, since the position of a vehicle ultimately depends on the doubly-integrated non-field specific force acting on it.

D

Geometry and gravitational fields

Strictly speaking, there is only one gravitational field, and it is ascribable to all the masses in the universe. Any convenient definition of a local field must take into account the location and magnitude of all significant nearby masses (the field of a single, isolated point mass decreases as $1/r^2$ with distance r). Near the earth's surface, for example, the only salient mass is taken to be that of the earth itself; clearly, in interplanetary space, the matter would not necessarily be so simple. In any case, it should be noted that *the field may be represented by a three-dimensional spatial distribution of force vectors,* and that the navigation

Observation	Conclusion of Observer Outside of Elevator	Conclusion of Observer Inside of Elevator
Test mass at rest with respect to elevator.	Elevator falling freely in unit gravitational field at one gravity acceleration.[1]	Elevator an acceleration-free system.
Test mass falls at one gravity acceleration with respect to elevator.	Elevator at rest. Mass falling freely in unit gravitational field.[2]	Elevator moving upward at one gravity acceleration.
Test mass falls at two gravities acceleration with respect to elevator.	Elevator moving upward at one gravity acceleration. Mass falling freely in unit gravitational field.	Elevator moving upward at two gravities acceleration.

[1] An acceleration of one gravity equals 980 centimeters/(second)^2.

[2] A unit gravitational field is equivalent to one-gravity acceleration.

Summary 4-1. Elevator example of equivalence of gravitational and inertial effects.

system may be regarded as moving (in general, accelerating) through this vector field, with the onboard accelerometers reading indistinguishably the vector sum of gravitation and force per unit mass (specific force) propelling the vehicle. (Actually, they read the negative of this specific force, since the accelerometers themselves are moving through the field.)

Thus the *field geometry* is important to the navigator; his foreknowledge of the distribution of the field vectors he encounters is his only way of distinguishing his propulsive acceleration from the field.

The gravity field of the earth

Inertial navigation uses accelerometers in gyro-referred coordinates, and needs gravitational field data in order to interpret the accelerometer readings. Terrestrial inertial navigation is concerned particularly with the *gravitational* field of the earth, and also with its *gravity* field. These fields have already been distinguished: the gravity field is the vector sum of the gravitational field and the centrifugal specific force due to the (daily) inertial rotation of the earth. This angular velocity of rotation will be called *earth rate*, and for terrestrial navigation will be restricted to meaning, as a practical matter, the daily angular velocity of the earth about its polar axis, which, for inertial-navigation purposes, will be regarded as along a line fixed in inertial space. The period of the rotation is one *sidereal* day, whose duration is 23 hours, 56 minutes and 4.9 seconds, or less than 24 *mean solar* hours.

It is the direction of the gravity field which is commonly called the *vertical*, and which defines the *astronomic vertical*, the reference in astronomic measurements of star-position, and also of positions of points on the earth referred to stars. The gravity direction therefore defines the navigator's vertical.

There is at once a contradiction in terms, if the navigator accelerates (or even moves in certain directions at constant speed) over the earth's surface; for the vertical as defined always refers to the location of the gravity direction at a point stationary on the earth as it might be indicated by a plumb bob. Thus the navigator uses the surveyor's vertical as a conceptual reference, even though the navigator must stand still on the earth to have this vertical indicated to him independently of any prespecification of the gravity field.

The shape of the earth: the geoid

To say that the direction of the vertical is known at the earth's surface is to say that the shape of the earth's gravity field equipotential is known. The shape is to first approximation a sphere; but higher-order approximations are more difficult to arrive at.

If the earth were a non-rotating fluid mass, the surface of minimum potential energy would indeed be a sphere. But the earth's daily rotation causes it to bulge in the equatorial region, in such a way that the centrifugal force is balanced by internal forces, and the resulting shape is nearly, but not quite, an ellipsoid of revolution. If the earth were a rotating fluid with its present mass distribution, it would be smoother than it is in fact: the shape so hypothesized is called that of *the geoid* (Fig. 4-2). The surface of the geoid is of mean sea level. A network of narrow canals cut through the continents would in principle allow the geoid surface to be determined everywhere on the earth.

The geoid is thus empirically determined; it takes the mass distribution of the earth as given; and it cannot in general correspond exactly to an ellipsoid, which is an analytic figure. The geoid is not describable by an equation from analytic geometry, although the ellipsoid nearest to it is. It turns out that the surface of that ellipsoid which appears to be the best approximation to the geoid departs from the geoid surface by

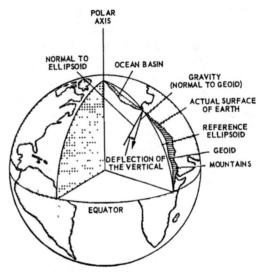

Fig. 4-2. Relationship of the geoid and a reference ellipsoid.

about one per cent of the topographic variations in the elevation of the earth's crust (due to mountains, ocean deeps, etc.). The definition of the geoid makes it one of the equipotential surfaces of the earth's gravity field, and the astronomic vertical is everywhere perpendicular to the geoid surface.

The preceding reference to geoid elevation and to ocean deeps deserves amplification. As an extreme example of the latter, the ocean deep off Puerto Rico may be cited: gravity there departs from its expected value in terms of a reference ellipsoid (the Hayford ellipsoid, to be described shortly) by about 300 milligals, where a milligal is defined as one-millionth of a gravity, or about 0.001 cm/sec². The corresponding depth of the 'dent' in the geoid is about 34 meters.[13]

It is common to locate islands in the sea by means of astronomic measurements based on the direction of the local gravity vector, rather than geodetic survey. The location of these islands may be seriously in doubt in terms of continental survey references, and the expectation of irregularities in the magnitude (and therefore the direction) of gravity is not lessened by the fact that such islands are usually themselves large mass-anomalies on the earth's surface. The application of land-based radiation measurements like Shoran to this problem is useful in tying such astronomically measured points in with the nearest geodetic continental grid. Even a continental survey assumes this insular character with respect to some of the other continental grids, and it is a function of radiative devices—not yet realized—to tie together the various continental surveys of the earth.

The shape of the earth: the approximating ellipsoid

It is to be expected that the ellipsoidal approximation to the geoid will have a circular cross-section at the equator, and that the normal to the surface of the ellipsoid and normal to the geoid will be nearly, but not quite, coincident. A global navigator, dependent on the ellipsoid as on a map, might thus determine his position erroneously if he placed in correspondence the normal to the ellipsoid at some indicated position and his own local astronomical vertical. The subject of this section is the selection of an ellipsoid which minimized these errors in vertical indication for position computation.

The basis of this effort to find the optimum ellipsoid is summarized in a publication[14] of the U.S. Coast and Geodetic Survey. The problem is *not* seen from the point of view of getting the ellipsoid whose normals are the best approximation to the set of astronomical verticals. The connection between the geometry and physics of the problem has, instead, been established by measuring the magnitude of the specific force of gravity on the earth's crust and then relating these measurements, by computation, to the values that would obtain on the geoid, i.e., at mean sea level. In this way the *elevation* of the geoid above some hypothesized analytic surface is computable: this analytic surface, generated by a process of three-dimensional curve-fitting, is the international reference ellipsoid.

In current practice, the words 'international reference ellipsoid', 'reference ellipsoid' and 'Hayford ellipsoid' are frequently used interchangeably. The process of arriving at a reference ellipsoid starts with a *geodetic survey*, which takes into account the curvature of the earth's surface (the so-called *land survey*, which is used to determine the boundaries of tracts, implies a flat earth). A geodetic survey is based on the measurements of nearly-spherical triangles on the earth's surface. As many contiguous triangles as possible start with a single base line; thus, the Hayford ellipsoid is based on a triangulation net covering the area of the United States. Note the purely geometric basis of the ellipsoid: it is obtained by the rotating of arcs through measured angles.

Value of the spherical earth-model

For practical navigational purposes, the earth is sufficiently close to a sphere so that departures from sphericity can be treated as small corrections. For this purpose the ellipticity (or *flattening* or *compression*) of the reference ellipsoid, is defined by

$$e \equiv \frac{a-b}{a}$$

where e is the ellipticity of any meridian section ellipse, a is the semi-major axis, and b the semi-minor axis. In geodetic surveying, e is only about one part in 297, so that the *deviation* D_{nR} of the ellipsoid normal from a spherical radius, or angle measured from the radius to the normal, is approximated by

$$D_{nR} \cong e \sin 2L_a$$

where L_a is the astronomical latitude. The angle D_{nR} is a smooth, computable function of latitude, and accounts completely for the departure of reference ellipsoid from a sphere, in navigation. The maximum value of D_{nR} is about 11.5 minutes of arc, at a latitude of plus-or-minus 45 degrees.

Insofar as the geoid does not follow the ellipsoid, the normals to the ellipsoidal surface will not be along the vertical. These departures of the space gradient of the gravity vector from analyticity are of the order of about 0.25 minute of arc (over a continental land mass) and are irregular in direction and magnitude. This small angle, measured from the ellipsoid normal to the gravity vector direction, is called the *deflection of the vertical* in geodetic survey work. The departure of gravity in magnitude or direction from its expected value on the ellipsoid surface is called, in general, the *gravity anomaly*. The deflections of the vertical are non-analytic and therefore unpredictable except by actual measurements and subsequent computations. In the absence of a highly precise gravity survey aimed at plotting gravity anomalies, these deflections of the vertical represent a basic substratum of uncertainty in vertical indication for navigational purposes.

It will be seen in addition that the presence of gravity anomalies along some course on which a vehicle is in motion will have the effect of swinging around the direction of the local gravity field in which the vehicle finds itself, and this rotation will not be smooth and predictable but erratic and unpredictable. Thus, for an inertial navigation system, the gravity anomalies acquire the character of 'white' *noise*, in the sense in which servo engineers use the term. This is in line with the previous statement that navigation converts space derivatives of force into time derivatives; here, space 'frequencies' of gravity deflections are converted to conventional time-frequencies. In this light, the determination of gravity anomalies themselves from moving vehicles is a difficult undertaking. It requires precise representation of the geometry in which force measurements can be made, and also precise independently-derived information about the non-field forces on the vehicle. Thus far, precise gravity (magnitude) measurement, or *gravimetry*, has been confined to locations stationary on the earth or under special conditions at sea (e.g., in submarines).

Other analytical approximations to the earth's gravity field have been proposed at various times. The most common is the sphere or point-mass field, and if a thin ring of mass be added in a region somewhat inside the equator, the elliptic quality of the equipotential surfaces can be reproduced. These matters are discussed in the literature.[15]

Large-scale mapping

The question of the optimum reference-figure for precise navigation on the earth is far from settled. Since the specification of destination for missile-type vehicles depends on such a 'map' in the same sense as ship navigation depends on navigator's charts, the importance of the specification of the optimum reference ellipsoid is clear. It was noted that the Hayford ellipsoid is based on a geodetic survey of the United States alone. In the absence of ocean surveys, it would be possible for disjunct survey nets on other continents to yield differing reference ellipsoidal surfaces, with fictitious discontinuities between them. To assure that gravity observations form a self-consistent set, the calibration of gravimeters—i.e., refined spring balances—with respect to a single reference location must be maintained over long travel times, in the present state of the art. The single reference point has been taken arbitrarily to be in the Geodetic Institute at Potsdam, Germany. Gravity magnitudes are usually referred to this point, for which the standard value is, at the present time, 981.2633 cm/sec². It would be highly desirable if world-wide gravity magnitude measurements could be made that, reduced to the geoid, had a relative accuracy of about 0.001 cm/sec², an ideal not yet attained.[16]

CHAPTER 5

GUIDANCE SYSTEM CONFIGURATIONS, FORCE TRACKING AND SCHULER TUNING

Instrumented coordinates

The inertial navigation problem is solved by instruments which may be thought of as having coordinate systems embedded in them. Thus, triads of gyros (Fig. 3-3) and of accelerometers serve as instrumented models for the ideal vehicle-centered coordinates already discussed. These actual instruments must be distinguished carefully from their ideal counterparts, because the quantitative measures of the performance of a navigation device is a set of angles, angular velocities and angular velocity derivatives of the instrumented axes with respect to the ideal-reference axes.

Instrumented coordinates have significance in three kinds of operation in navigation systems:

1. *Measurement* of specific force on the vehicle.
2. *Computation* to distinguish the gravitational field from the propulsive and drag forces on the vehicle.
3. *Position Indication*, in which the course is presented to the navigator purely geometrically, as on a map.

The role of gyros is, as has been observed, to aid in setting up a model of a reference coordinate system. This may be the coordinate system in which position is measured or the coordinate system in which force is measured (a distinction which separates inertial guidance systems into two classes); or the gyros may serve as a model of the single coordinate system in which both force measurement and position measurement take place, as in missile guidance and proposed extraterrestrial guidance systems. Thus three broad classes of inertial guidance systems emerge, based on the disposition of accelerometers and gyros in the gimbaled instrumented coordinates.

A typical gyro package making up one such instrumented coordinate

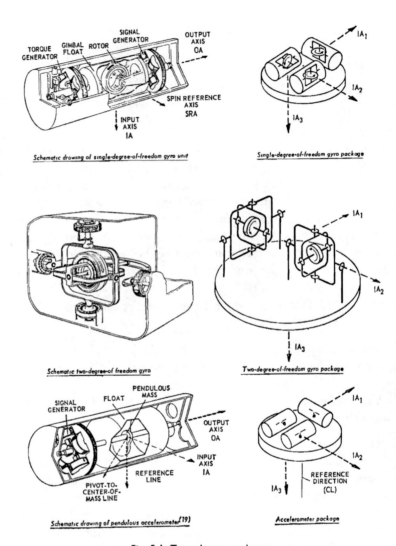

Fig. 5-1. Typical gyro packages.

system may consist fundamentally of three single-degree-of-freedom integrating gyros (Fig. 5-1a) or two two-degree-of-freedom gyros (Fig. 5-1b). These units, as well as rate gyros, are treated in Chapter 7, as is also the coupling of the gyro units with the associated follow-up servo to produce a *space integrator*. As observed in Chapter 3, this last-named device combines two functions: an integrating drive, and geometrical isolation of an inertial-space-referred instrument coordinate system from the motions of the vehicle in roll, pitch and yaw. This results in a drive that integrates with respect to inertial space. The sensitive, or input, axes of the gyro units determine a reference coordinate frame fixed in the gyro package.

The accelerometer package, used to measure forces, consists in general of three single-axis accelerometers; but if vertical accelerations are small compared to gravity, two accelerometers suffice. Each accelerometer (Fig. 5-1c) responds to mass forces (gravitation plus inertial reaction) along its sensitive or *input* axis. These sensitive axes are made mutually orthogonal. (Two-axis accelerometers, or single- or two-axis pendulums, might also be used.) When two single-axis units are used, the line normal to the plane determined by their input axes becomes the controlled line for a vertical indicating system; this line is called the indicated vertical. Figure 5-1c illustrates an accelerometer package. Accelerometers and pendulums are treated at length by various authors.[17, 18] In Fig. 5-1c, the accelerometer shown in the schematic drawing is a single-degree-of-freedom floated pendulum.

Reference coordinate storage: geometric storage

A gyro package may be used with two distinct types of reference coordinate storage: the *geometric* and the *analytic*. In the geometric storage method, the gyro package, physically representing the reference coordinate system, remains—as nearly as possible—fixed in inertial space, while the rest of the system, including the vehicle, rotates around it. The mechanical decoupling between the gyros and the surrounding gimbals and vehicle frame is accomplished by servo drives. In this kind of system (Fig. 3-8), the gyro package remains non-rotating relative to inertial space, mechanically decoupled from its environment; the gyro package coordinates are inertial. The accelerometer package indicates the vertical geometrically relative to the gyro package. In order that force measurements may be made in earth coordinates, a gimbal is set in rotation at the earth's daily angular rate about a line parallel to the earth's polar axis and passing through the inertial-reference package. Such a system was discussed as an example in Chapter 3. This kind of system is readily adapted to terrestrial airborne, marine and submarine navigation.

Analytic storage

In an analytically-storing system, the navigation reference directions are stored as numerical quantities representing angular displacement component signals with respect to the reference axes; the axes themselves never appear explicitly in the system. The numerical quantities are stored on electrical or electromechanical integrators as bias signals. In

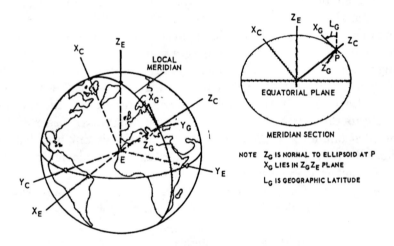

Fig. 5-2. Local geographic reference frame, latitude–longitude grid.

this scheme, the gyro package is no longer fixed with respect to inertial space. Instead, the gyros in the package are precessed in a controlled manner, so that the gyro package itself has an angular velocity with respect to inertial space (Fig. 1-6). The record of this gyro precession, stored on integrators, and properly modified for the effect of the earth's daily rotation, gives the required position angles. This kind of system is especially adaptable to measurements of force and position in geographic coordinates (Fig. 5-2).

There is another choice possible here: the gyros can be fixed in inertial space (as in geometric storage of the reference coordinates) while the vertical is indicated analytically, rather than physically, on the basis of force measurements made with inertially-mounted accelerometers (Fig. 5-3). Here the vertical is *computed* as a set of direction cosines in instrumented inertial coordinates. This type of system is natural for use in missile guidance, although it is not restricted to this field.

The position computation

The objective in measuring the specific force is to compute with its aid the acceleration of the vehicle on and across course. In general, the

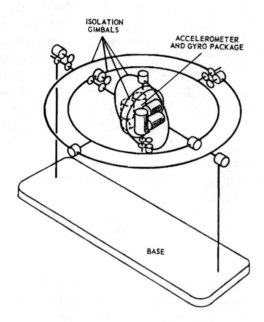

Fig 5-3. Accelerometer package fixed to gyro package, which is inertial.

total specific force on any vehicle is the negative vector sum of the non-field forces acting on the vehicle, e.g., lift, drag, and thrust. The identification of lift is dependent on a knowledge of the gravitational field in which the vehicle is operating as well as the vehicle's acceleration in the direction of the field. Gravitation is distinguished in the measured specific force by a (feedback) computation, as are also any forces due to the measurement in rotating coordinates. The remainder, the acceleration on course, is then doubly-integrated to get position (Fig. 5-4).

It will be clear that indicated position and velocity must be known in advance if the above computation is to take place, but as these quantities are also to be derived from the computation, the computation must be a closed-loop process. Moreover, the identification of the gravitational field is also part of the problem of position indication; therefore this computation is a closed-loop process also. It follows that all inertial navigation systems must have this closed-loop characteristic.

Since the inertial guidance device measures the total force on the vehicle, its interpretation of this measurement in terms of course and position must be somewhat different from the conventional view. Thus, a ship moving over the earth would be seen by an inertially-fixed observer as an object moving in roll, pitch and yaw about some center of rotation, while this center simultaneously moves along a curve in space. The curvature is very nearly that of the earth when the ship is on a steady course and steaming east or west; but for other courses the curvature may be a much more complex function of position on the earth, and of time. Thus the earth's rotation must also be 'seen' by inertial-guidance equipment if the total force measurement is to be interpreted ultimately as a displacement over the earth. An independently-obtained knowledge of the time, i.e., of the earth's daily angular velocity, is needed in this interpretation. Finally, the direction and magnitude of the earth's gravitational field must be known as a function of every point on the course.

Thus, there are three categories of effort in the design of inertial guidance systems—gyros, accelerometers, and velocity and/or position computers.

The final problem is that of automatic steering; for many vehicles this may be regarded as a separate problem from that of developing position information from the inertially-referred force measurement; in others, particularly in aircraft or missiles, it becomes an integral part of the cross-course guidance system.

In all cases an accurate indication of the local vertical is required. Techniques for achieving this on a moving vehicle are discussed in the following sections.

Vertical indication methods

In non-automatic marine or aeronautical navigation, a sextant is leveled; and an artificial horizon, as used in aircraft, is also a device which indicates a level surface. These devices, when they are stationary with respect to the earth, indicate the *astronomic*, or *true vertical*, i.e., the

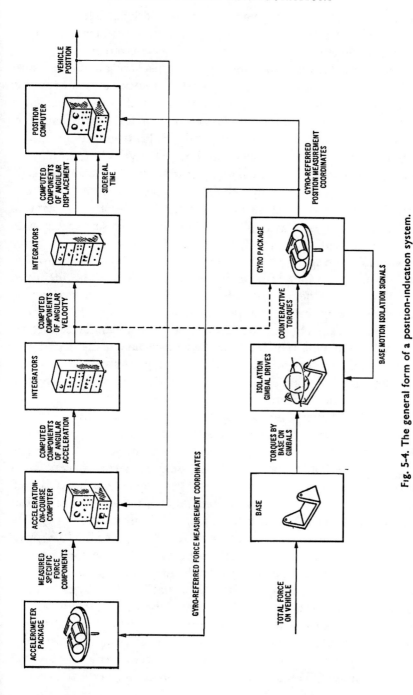

Fig. 5-4. The general form of a position-indication system.

local gravity direction. Astronomic latitude and longitude are defined in terms of this astronomic vertical. Thus, in an elementary way, a force measurement—gravity—is used to indicate position.

When these devices—essentially pendulums—are accelerated over the earth's surface, or even moved at constant velocity over the rotating non-spherical earth by the vehicle carrying them, they will indicate not the gravity direction, but the direction of the total force acting on them. This total force is the sum of those due to gravity and the inertia reaction effects of the *inertial* acceleration of the vehicle (excluding in the latter the effect of centrifugal acceleration due to the earth's daily rotation, which is included by definition in gravity). In the absence of externally-derived data, these forces are indistinguishable. If data on the environment are available—barometric pressure, speed with respect to the medium of travel, distance to landmarks, etc.—the force components making up the total force may be separable, to within certain approximations. In particular, if gravity can be identified separately from kinematic acceleration, one axis of a geographic coordinate system can be approximated: the geographic vertical. Notice that the direction of the astronomic vertical cannot be directly measured in a moving vehicle; it constitutes raw data, as compared with the geographic vertical, which is based on a hypothesized earth-model. Only the geographic model is analytic, and can thus be a direction resulting from the mechanized computation.

The other two axes of a geographic coordinate system, east–west and north–south, are in the horizontal plane, and are arrived at instrumentally by rotation of a compass indicator of some kind. A magnetic compass needle fails to point along geographic north, in general; a gyrocompass does tend to point along geographic north, as is well known. In fact, a gyrocompass utilizes its own pendulosity as well as its large rotational momentum to track, simultaneously, both gravity and the earth's daily rotational angular velocity vector (the polar axis). Thus a gyrocompass is a prototype of the instrumentation of a geographic coordinate model. Although adequately accurate for its purposes at marine speeds, it is only a partial inertial system in comparison with the inertial-navigation devices discussed in this book.

The artificial-horizon technique for indicating the vertical uses a flat-earth model; that is, gravity is assumed to be constant in direction, while accelerations are considered to average to zero over a time interval of a few minutes. Thus, such an indicator of the vertical becomes effectively a geometrical (mechanical) low-pass filter.[17] The difficulty in constructing a mechanical filter with a time parameter of several minutes resulted in devices with an accuracy of about one-half degree in normal level flight operation and of many degrees during maneuvers; this is only moderate accuracy, by present-day standards. Isolation from roll, pitch and yaw interferences on measurement is considerably better than isolation from maneuver effects since the fundamental periods of roll, pitch and yaw (a few seconds) are much shorter than the time parameter of the instrument whereas those of the maneuvers of the craft (a few minutes) are of the same order as the time parameter.

Schuler-tuning of a pendulum

Any more precise treatment of the indication of the vertical from moving bases uses the concept of a geocentrically rotating vertical. This was first recognized by Schuler in his classic paper;[3] he expresses the acceleration of a point near the surface of a hypothetical spherical earth in terms of geocentric angular motion of the earth radius to the point.

On a vehicle moving over a spherical earth, the local vertical at the vehicle's instantaneous position rotates geocentrically with respect to the earth at an angular rate numerically equal in minutes of arc per hour to the vehicle ground speed in knots. A pendulum in the vehicle would have to rotate with respect to the earth at a constant angular velocity in order to indicate the vertical continuously. Once it was brought up to speed, no torque would be required to keep the pendulum along the vertical during this rotation. On the other hand, if the vehicle were to accelerate, by changing either speed or heading, a torque would be required to maintain the pendulum on the geocentrically-accelerating vertical.

Schuler[3] pointed out in 1923 that, assuming the earth to be a sphere and having a pendulum initially aligned with the local earth radius, accurate indication of the vertical even during periods of acceleration could be realized by suitable choice of the natural period of the pendulum. Whenever the pivot of a pendulum is accelerated, the center of mass of the pendulum tends to 'lag behind' the pivot, with respect to inertial coordinates. At the same time, this acceleration causes the true vertical, which, under the simplifying assumptions used in this treatment, is a line through the center of the earth and the pivot, to undergo a geocentric angular acceleration with respect to inertial space. The

E

rotational sense of these two motions is the same. These considerations lead to the following observation:

> If a pendulum initially hangs vertically, it will remain along the vertical if, as seen from inertial space, *its angular acceleration about its pivot equals the geocentric angular acceleration of the vertical.*

These two angular accelerations become equal for a distributed-mass pendulum when the ratio of the displacement of the center of mass from the pivot to the square of the radius of gyration of the pendulum equals the reciprocal of the radius of the earth. When the pendulum is operating undamped in the earth's gravity field, this condition gives the pendulum a natural period of oscillation of approximately eighty-four minutes, and the pendulum is said to be *Schuler-tuned*. For a shorter-period pendulum the rotation-producing torque on the pendulous element about its pivot is stronger, so the pendulum angularly-accelerates too rapidly and lags the vertical. For a longer-period pendulum the torque is weaker and the pendulum leads the true vertical. This Schuler-tuning condition is presented in Fig. 5-5.

An equivalent simulation of a Schuler pendulum by servo techniques

An 84 minute period is very long compared to the periods of physical pendulums ordinarily encountered. In fact, it is improbable that a simple (concentrated mass) pendulum or a distributed-mass pendulum could be constructed with this period.[3, 4] In practical cases an equivalent pendulum is obtained by feedback techniques. A condition analogous to the Schuler tuning of a pendulum is realized in a closed-loop system wherein accelerometers track the force on the vehicle, and the orientation of a gimballed package supporting the accelerometers is controlled by signals derived from the accelerometer measurements. The package itself is then an equivalent Schuler-tuned pendulum. A line inscribed in the package indicates the earth-radius; or, more exactly (excluding gravity anomaly effects), the geographic vertical. The addition of control of the package in azimuth then permits a local geographic coordinate system to be indicated by axes inscribed on the package.

Design of a Schuler-tuned package

The design of a simulated Schuler pendulum has far more flexibility

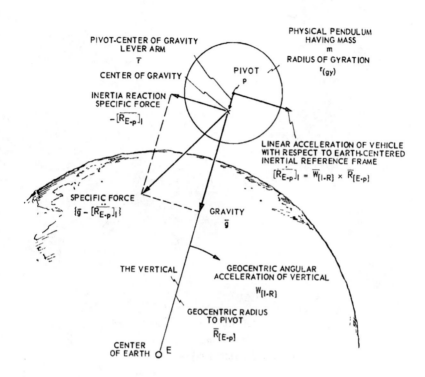

IDEAL SITUATION

ARM $\bar{r}$ REMAINS PARALLEL TO GRAVITY $\bar{g}$

NONROTATING SPHERICAL EARTH ASSUMED FOR SIMPLICITY (DOES NOT INVALIDATE RESULTS)

APPLIED TORQUE DUE TO ACCELERATION $= m\bar{r} \times \{-[\overline{R_{E-p}}]_I\} = mr\,R_{[E-p]}\overline{W}_{[I-R]}$

INERTIA REACTION OF PENDULUM $= mr^2_{(gy)}\overline{W}_{[I-p]}$

$$mr^2_{(gy)}\overline{W}_{[I-p]} = mr\,R_{[E-p]}\overline{W}_{[I-R]}$$

FOR SCHULER TUNING, THE ANGULAR ACCELERATION OF THE PENDULUM MUST EQUAL THE GEOCENTRIC ANGULAR ACCELERATION OF THE VERTICAL, I.E.,

$$\overline{W}_{[I-p]} = \overline{W}_{[I-R]}$$

SO THAT $\boxed{\dfrac{r}{r^2_{(gy)}} = \dfrac{1}{R_{[E-p]}}}$ IS THE SCHULER TUNING CONDITION.

a) Schuler tuning condition in terms of physical-pendulum dimensions

Fig. 5-5 Simplified derivation of the Schuler tuning condition on a physical pendulum. (Page I of 2)

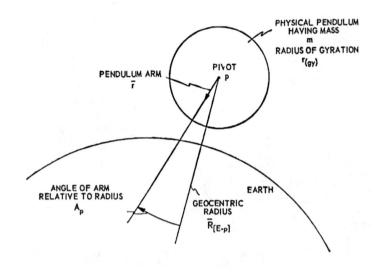

GENERAL SITUATION

ARM $\bar{r}$ NOT PARALLEL TO GRAVITY $\bar{g}$

APPLIED TORQUE $= m\bar{r} \times \{\bar{g} - [\overline{R_{E-p}}]_i\}$

$$= m r \, R_{[E-p]} \ddot{\overline{W}}_{[I-R]} - m r g \, \overline{A}_p$$

INERTIA REACTION OF PENDULUM $= m r^2_{(gy)} \ddot{\overline{W}}_{[I-p]}$

$$= m r^2_{(gy)} \{\ddot{\overline{W}}_{[I-R]} + \ddot{\overline{A}}_p\}$$

$$\overline{A}_p + \frac{g r}{r^2_{(gy)}} \overline{A}_p = \left[\frac{r R_{[E-p]}}{r^2_{(gy)}} - 1 \right] \ddot{\overline{W}}_{[I-R]}$$

BY SCHULER TUNING (THAT IS, $\dfrac{r}{r^2_{(gy)}} = \dfrac{1}{R_{[E-p]}}$),

$$\ddot{\overline{A}}_p + \frac{g}{R_{[E-p]}} \overline{A}_p = 0$$

SCHULER PERIOD

$$T_{ns} = 2\pi \sqrt{\frac{R_{[E-p]}}{g}} = 84.6 \text{ MINUTES}$$

b) Period of a schuler-tuned pendulum

Fig. 5-5. Simplified derivation of the Schuler tuning condition on a physical pendulum. (Page 2 of 2)

than has the design of a physical pendulum, because in the simulated pendulum the force-measuring properties are separate from the torque-producing properties. These properties appear in two distinct subsystems linked by some dynamic control function. The vertical indicator is thus composed of:

(a) A force-measuring subsystem: this is an assemblage of accelerometers, which measures the force on the vehicle in instrumented geographic coordinates.

(b) A torque-producing subsystem: this is either a torqued gyro package (representing the instrumented geographic axes) which supports the force-measuring subsystem directly, or a set of integrating drives which operate between a gyro package (representing instrumented inertial axes) and the force-measuring subsystem (which then represents the instrumented geographic axes).

(c) A dynamic control coupling between the accelerometer output and the integrating drive inputs.

In the case of a linear system the performance parameters in the design may be conveniently expressed as damping ratios, natural frequencies, and characteristic times.[20]

The force-measuring subsystem indicates the resultant specific force acting on the vertical indicator. When the vertical indicator is accelerated over the earth, this force is no longer aligned with gravity, which it is desired to track. The specific force is along the *apparent vertical*, while gravity is along the *true vertical*. Thus, vertical indication on an accelerated craft presents the peculiar problem of indicating the direction of gravity by means of a device that can actually track only the resultant force acting on the tracking element.

The principle of operation

The operation of an equivalent Schuler-tuned pendulum can be understood from the analysis of a simplified, single-axis model of a gimballed package. Suppose it is required to operate in a vehicle moving over a spherical nonrotating earth. The vehicle maintains constant altitude, but, in general, is accelerated tangentially to its path. This single-axis treatment, which is detailed in Derivation Summary 6-1 in Chapter 6, provides a background for the more general case of a vehicle moving in unrestricted fashion over a spheroidal rotating earth. The equation of motion of the Schuler-tuned package is similar to that of a simple pendulum of undamped natural period of 84 minutes, approximately; and it is, as well, the 'error equation' of an undamped servo loop with the same natural period. Thus, a physical pendulum of unmanageably long period has been simulated by a servo loop with a period at the disposal of the designer. Further, when on an accelerating vehicle, this servo loop positions a line—the indicated vertical, inscribed on the controlled member—to coincide with the local vertical determined by a hypothesized earth-model. Thus, under these conditions the simulated Schuler pendulum oscillates about a hypothesized vertical direction, as, indeed, a physical Schuler pendulum would do if it could be constructed. The control of this oscillation is a servo problem, the subject of Chapter 6.

SCHULER TUNING AND DAMPING OF A VERTICAL INDICATING SYSTEM

IN A vertical indication loop the force-measuring subsystem exerts dynamic control over the torque-producer. The coupling between these subsystems controls the dynamic correction angle between the indicated vertical and the true vertical, that is, it determines the frequency response of the loop. In the design of such a vertical indicating loop, the coupling is chosen to permit damping of oscillations without detuning the Schuler operation sufficiently to produce unacceptably large forced dynamic errors. Typical coupling devices between the force-measuring and torque-producing subsystems include:

(a) A direct nondynamic coupler.
(b) An integrator.
(c) An integrator and bypass, which acts as integration paralleled with lead (relative to the integrator output).
(d) An integrator combined with lead-lag operation.

While the assumption of single-axis operation is used here to simplify the analysis, the complete three-axis system with its interaxial coupling, as the actual case, must eventually be considered in any practical design. In practice, the results of linear theory arrived at using the methods of this chapter may be finally revised in terms of the feedback system behavior displayed by a three-axis non-linear mathematical simulation of the system on an automatic computer.

The linear theory required for the initial design study of the simplified Schuler-tuned single-axis vertical indicating system, shown pictorially in Fig. 6-1, is given in Chapter 5. Figure 6-2 is drawn to display the steady-state frequency response of such a system for forcing inputs in the form of velocities of the vehicle. In this figure the ratio of forcing frequency to Schuler frequency appears along the horizontal axis, while on the vertical axis is plotted the ratio of the number of minutes of arc

of correction to the indicated vertical to be expected for each knot*
of ground speed.

The four cases of accelerometer-to-gyro coupling cited above
correspond to the curves of Fig. 6-2. The curves are plotted from performance equations derived from Figs. 6-3, 6-4 and 6-5, which represent
in loop drawings the most useful coupling functions between accelerom-

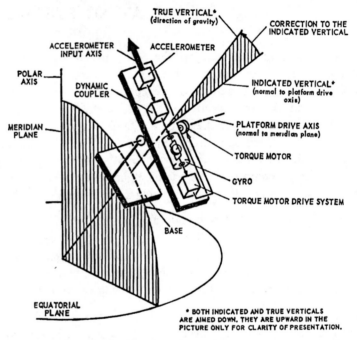

Fig. 6-1. Schematic diagram of a single-axis vertical indicating system constrained to
move in a meridian plane.

eter and gyro. The equations for each case may be summarized as
follows, in the order previously used:

(a) A system describable by a first-order differential equation. The
angle measured from the indicated vertical to the true vertical, *the
correction to the indicated vertical,* is the dependent variable and time is
the independent variable. One integration process, provided by the
space integrator, is present in the loop. This system in operation
resembles a pendulum that is heavily overdamped with respect to
inertial space.

* A knot is a nautical mile per hour; tangent to the earth's surface, it is equivalent to a
geocentric angular velocity of one minute of arc per hour.

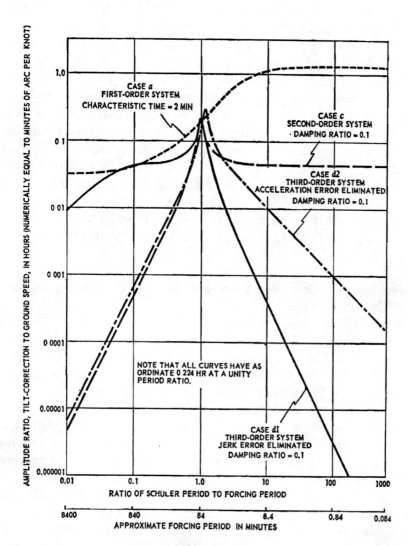

Fig. 6-2 Steady-state amplitude ratio—period ratio response for Schuler-tuned vertical indication loops.

(b) A second-order undamped system, which resembles an undamped pendulum in operation.

(c) A second-order damped system, which resembles in operation a pendulum damped with respect to the total specific force vector.

(d) A third-order damped system, which resembles in operation a pendulum damped to inertial space by the so-called 'differentiated tachometer feedback' type of damping, although no tachometers or differentiators as such are actually present; the derived signal modification is obtained by proper phase control in the coupling device. The criteria for preferring one of these methods over the others involve the choice of components, the specified operating time, the derived accuracy, the complexity permitted in the design, the requirement for damping, and the effects of the smoothing of data incurred in damping. The overriding consideration, however, may well be the effect of forced errors. This last is discussed, in what follows, in terms of the equations for the various single-axis vertical indication loops in cases (a), (b), (c), and (d) above.

Direct coupling between force-measurer and torque producer (Case 'a')

A nondynamic or direct coupler, such as a wideband amplifier, is inserted between the force-measuring subsystem and the torque-producing subsystem. The latter, as has been observed, is functionally a space integrator; since the other components of the loop are nondynamic, the performance is describable by a first-order differential equation. A device of this type is often called an *artificial horizon*, which may be regarded as the first-order system resulting from heavily overdamping a pendulum. The system is subject to forced dynamic errors due to both velocity and acceleration of the craft. The seriousness of the velocity error is determined by the tightness of coupling between force-measurer and space integrator: the stronger the coupling, the smaller the velocity error. The acceleration error is independent of coupling strength, once the forcing period exceeds a certain value, and is approximately the ratio of craft acceleration to gravity—the same error displayed by any short-period pendulum, reflecting its tendency to track the direction of the total force acting on it (the direction of the apparent vertical) rather than the true vertical. The artificial horizon is a good indicator of the vertical when it is on a craft that is subject only to roll, pitch and yaw, provided the craft moves in normal straight-line flight, but it becomes poor when the craft maneuvers. Its performance, which is discussed in case (a) of Derivation Summary 6-2, is not adequate for inertial guidance. Note that this system, being non-oscillatory, cannot be Schuler-tuned.

Single-integrator coupling between force-measurer and torque producer (Case 'b')

When the coupling is through an integrator, so that the integrator output is the space integrator input, the system performance is of second order and undamped, exhibiting, in general, an acceleration error. This forced dynamic error is, however, a function of the natural period of the pendulum, as observed in Chapter 5, in the case of the physical pendulum, and the error may be nulled by selecting the Schuler period (about 84 minutes) as the natural period. In the physical-pendulum case this appears to be physically impossible as a mechanical adjustment. However, setting the undamped natural period of a pendulum is quite different from setting the corresponding period into a feedback loop, because of the greater number of controllable parameters in the latter, and because in a feedback loop, the period-setting is a gain-control adjustment. Thus the equivalent pendulum comprising practical components can be Schuler-tuned.

The equation of motion of a Schuler-tuned vertical indicator can be derived from two points of view, as is done in Derivation Summary 6-1. From the first viewpoint, the Schuler-tuning adjustment consists of putting a calibrated dynamic lag into the system, so that the indicated vertical lags the apparent vertical, which in turn geometrically leads the true vertical. By proper calibration, i.e., Schuler tuning, the dynamic lag can be matched to the geometrical lead. From the second point of view, an inherent tracking aid is properly calibrated for the system when it is Schuler-tuned, so that the acceleration input is an inherent lead compensation which can be made to annul the dynamic lag between indicated and true verticals. These approaches are, of course, but two different views of a single problem, that of rendering tangential accelerations of the vertical indicator on an assumed spherical earth helpful and necessary rather than disturbing. The conclusions apply equally to mechanical pendulums.

Integrator-and-bypass coupling: Damping (Case 'c')

If the configuration of the previous section has a bypass added around

Schuler Tuning as a Calibrated Dynamic Lag

To show how Schuler tuning corresponds in its effects to a calibrated dynamic lag in a vertical indicator, first define the *correction to the indicated vertical with respect to the apparent vertical* $[\overline{(C)V}]_{(a,i)}$ as the rotation that would have to be applied to the indicated vertical to align it with the apparent vertical. Then

$$[\overline{(C)V}]_{(a,i)} \equiv \overline{I}_{Vi} \times \overline{I}_{Va}\, q_{(a,i)} \tag{1}$$

where

$\overline{I}_{Vi} \equiv$ unit vector along the indicated vertical

$\overline{I}_{Va} \equiv$ unit vector along the apparent vertical $\qquad ; \qquad q_{(a,i)} \equiv \dfrac{[(C)V]_{(a,i)}}{\sin\,[(C)V]_{(a,i)}}$

This is a *vector angle*; its rate of change with respect to the earth is[*]

$$\{p\,[\overline{(C)V}]_{(a,i)}\}_E = \overline{W}_{(EV)a} - \overline{W}_{(EV)i} \tag{2}$$

where

$\overline{W}_{(EV)a} \equiv$ angular velocity of the apparent vertical relative to the earth

$\overline{W}_{(EV)i} \equiv$ angular velocity of the indicated vertical relative to the earth

From the vertical indicator loop, Fig. 6-3,[**]

$$\overline{W}_{(EV)i} = S_{(Vi)[f;\dot{W}]}\frac{1}{p}\,(\overline{I}_{Vi}\times\overline{f}) + \overline{W}_{[(EV)i]_0} \tag{3}$$

where

$S_{(Vi)[f;\dot{W}]} = S_{(sfr)[f;e]}\, S_{(int)[e;i]}\, S_{(si)[i;W]}$
= the vertical indicator sensitivity, the product of specific force receiver, integrator and drive sensitivities

$S_{(sfr)[f;e]}$ = specific force receiver sensitivity

$S_{(int)[e;i]}$ = signal integrator sensitivity

$S_{(si)[i;W]}$ = space integrator sensitivity

$\overline{f}$ is the total specific force along the apparent vertical; thus

$$\overline{I}_{Va} \equiv \frac{\overline{f}}{f} \tag{4}$$

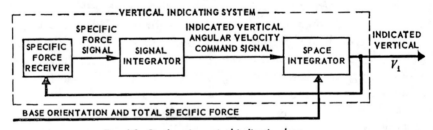

Fig. 6-3. Single-axis vertical indicating loop.

[*] Assuming that no rotation *about* the indicated vertical occurs, i.e., an azimuth control or compass operates to stabilize the vertical indicator about the vertical.

[**] Note that while the accelerometer actually responds to $[(\overline{I}_{Vi}\times\overline{f})\times\overline{I}_{Vi}]$, the drive is so oriented relative to the accelerometer that *it* responds to a function of $\overline{I}_{Vi}\times[(\overline{I}_{Vi}\times\overline{f})\times\overline{I}_{Vi}]$ which equals $(\overline{I}_{Vi}\times\overline{f})$, as given in the equation.

Derivation Summary 6-1. The Schuler tuning of a gravity tracker. (Page 1 of 3)

Note that

$$\bar{I}_{V1} \times \bar{f} = \bar{I}_{V1} \times \bar{I}_{Va} f = \frac{f \, \overline{[(C)V]}_{(a,1)}}{q_{(a,1)}} \qquad (5)$$

so that from the foregoing,

$$\left[p^2 + \frac{S_{(V1)[t;\dot{w}]} f}{q_{(a,1)}} \right] \overline{[(C)V]}_{(a,1)} = p \, \overline{W}_{(EV)a} \qquad (6)$$

This is the equation of motion for a system tracking the apparent vertical. Since the true vertical is desired, it is necessary to investigate the geometrical relationships between the apparent and true verticals. It is subsequently shown that, in the presence of accelerations, the apparent vertical leads the true vertical, i.e., its direction is parallel to the direction the true vertical will attain in the near future. The problem is to make the indicated vertical lag the apparent vertical by the same angle that the apparent vertical leads the true vertical. Define this latter angle $\bar{A}_{(t-a)}$ as

$$\bar{A}_{(t-a)} = \bar{I}_{Vt} \times \bar{I}_{Va} \, q_{(t,a)} \qquad (7)$$

and

$$[p\bar{A}_{(t-a)}]_E = \bar{W}_{(EV)a} - \bar{W}_{(EV)t} \qquad (8)$$

where

$$\bar{I}_{Vt} \equiv \frac{\bar{g}}{g} \cong -\frac{\bar{R}_E}{R_E}$$

$$q_{(t,a)} \equiv \frac{A_{(t-a)}}{\sin A_{(t-a)}}$$

$\bar{W}_{(EV)t} \equiv$ angular velocity of true vertical relative to the earth

$\bar{g} \equiv$ gravity

$\bar{R}_E \equiv$ the (assumed constant magnitude) earth-radius

The tangential acceleration of the vertical indicator* on the earth is considered to be

$$\bar{a} = p \, \bar{W}_{(EV)t} \times \bar{R}_E \qquad (9)$$

so that

$$\bar{f} = \bar{g} - \bar{a} = \bar{I}_{Vt} g - p \, \bar{W}_{(EV)t} \times \bar{R}_E \qquad (10)$$

Note that the inertia reaction effect of an acceleration is opposite in direction to the acceleration. The cross product of $\bar{I}_{Vt}$ into Eq. (10), gives $\bar{I}_{Vt} \times \bar{f} = R_E p \, \bar{W}_{(EV)t}$. Substitution of this into the derivative of Eq. (8), use of Eq. (7), and rearrangement of terms gives

$$p \, \bar{W}_{(EV)a} = \left[p^2 + \frac{f}{R_E \, q_{(t,a)}} \right] \bar{A}_{(t-a)} \qquad (11)$$

If the correction to the indicated vertical relative to the apparent vertical, or angle by which the indicated vertical lags the apparent vertical, is to equal the angle by which the apparent vertical leads the true vertical, i.e., if

$$\overline{[(C)V]}_{(a,1)} = \bar{A}_{(t-a)} \qquad (12)$$

---

* For the assumed condition of a spherical nonrotating earth (which simplifies the problem for demonstrating the Schuler effect without restricting its validity) the tangential acceleration is the only important acceleration term. The full equation is Eq. (2-3) in Derivation Summary 2, page 32 of reference 12.

Derivation Summary 6-1. The Schuler tuning of a gravity tracker. (Page 2 of 3)

it is necessary that, comparing Eqs. (6) and (11),

$$S_{(V1)[f;\dot{w}]} \equiv \frac{1}{R_s} = \frac{1}{R_E} \tag{13}$$

which is the Schuler tuning condition, where R_s is the Schuler radius.

Schuler Tuning as a Calibrated Tracking Aid

Schuler tuning can also be equated to the calibration of an inherent acceleration lead signal due to angular acceleration of the vertical indicator over an essentially spherical earth. This angular acceleration is actually then made useful in overcoming the lag of the apparent vertical behind the true vertical during accelerations. To see how this comes about, define

$$[\overline{(C)V}]_{(t,1)} \equiv \overline{I}_{V1} \times \overline{I}_{Vt} \tag{14}$$

where $q_{(t,1)}$ is practically unity, since $[(C)V]_{(t,1)}$ is a small angle. Note that (prohibiting rotation of the indicated about the true vertical by an ideal azimuth stabilizer, as before)

$$\{p\,[\overline{(C)V}]_{(t,1)}\}_E = \overline{W}_{(EV)t} - \overline{W}_{(EV)1} \tag{15}$$

while from Fig. 6-3, $\overline{W}_{(EV)1}$ is, as before, given by

$$\overline{W}_{(EV)1} = S_{(V1)[f;\dot{w}]} \frac{1}{p} (\overline{I}_{V1} \times \overline{f}) + \overline{W}_{[(EV)1]_0} \tag{16}$$

From the foregoing, including Eq. (10),

$$[p^2 + S_{(V1)[a;\dot{w}]}g]\,[\overline{(C)V}]_{(t,1)} = \underset{\substack{\uparrow \\ \text{lag}}}{\big[1} - \underset{\substack{\uparrow \\ \text{calibrated} \\ \text{(tracking aid)} \\ \text{lead}}}{S_{(V1)[f;\dot{w}]}R_E\big]}p\,\overline{W}_{(EV)t} \tag{17}$$

When the condition

$$S_{(V1)[f;\dot{w}]} \equiv \frac{1}{R_s} = \frac{1}{R_E} \tag{18}$$

is applied, the equation of motion of the vertical indicator is*

$$\Big[p^2 + \frac{g}{R_s}\Big]\,[\overline{(C)V}]_{(t,1)} = 0 \tag{19}$$

and the vertical indicator is Schuler tuned. This means that the second term in the right-hand side of Eq. (17), which represents calibration of the inherent acceleration lead, balances the first term that represents dynamic lag. This is a form of acceleration *tracking aid*.

---

* Strictly speaking, g should be replaced by the net vertical specific force: $f_V = g - a_V$.

Derivation Summary 6-1. The Schuler tuning of a gravity tracker. (Page 3 of 3)

the coupling integrator, the loop is damped and will settle down to a steady state, under favorable circumstances, when it is subject to uncaging errors or to transient disturbances. The gravity, i.e., tilt, component of the specific force signal appears as the elastic term via the integrator and as damping via the bypass. The acceleration component appears as the inherent tracking aid via the integrator but introduces an unwanted superfluous term via the bypass. This last term is the origin of the forced dynamic error peculiar to vertical indicators. The forced dynamic error is an acceleration derivative, or jerk, error tending to become predominant at frequencies high compared with the Schuler frequency, as is indicated in Derivation Summary 6-2, case (c). Forced errors due to damping may be minimized by injecting externally derived compensating inputs, with the effectiveness of the forced error cancellation determined by the accuracy of the compensation. The curve for case (c) in Fig. 6-2 applies to this kind of system.

Integrator-with-feedback cascaded with integrator-with-bypass coupling (Case 'd')

The above discussed integrator-with-bypass is sometimes called an integration-with-lead network which acts as a high-pass filter, and this section will deal with the addition of its low-pass counterpart, i.e., a lag network obtained by an integrator with nondynamic inverse feedback. This particular instrumentation of the lag network is required because of the long lag time needed.

As shown in Derivation Summary 6-2, the immediate result of this more elaborate coupling scheme is a choice of two Schuler-tuning methods; that is, the earth-radius can enter as a loop gain parameter in either of two ways. These are cases d1 and d2 respectively in Derivation Summary 6-2. In case (d1) the acceleration error will be eliminated, and the system is analogous to a Schuler-tuned physical pendulum. In case (d2), the jerk error is eliminated. Any attempt to eliminate both acceleration and jerk error together will result in undamping the system, as the lead and lag times would then be identical. The choice of Schuler tuning, then, reduces to a frequency response adjustment, and the frequency spectra of forced errors in the region of most probable disturbances become the largest determinants of loop-parameter values. The frequency response to forced errors for systems tuned by these methods is shown as cases (d1) and (d2) in Fig. 6-2. It should be noted that a Schuler-tuned vertical indicator always operates well into its

Given a single-axis vertical-indication loop (Fig. 6-3, Derivation Summary 6-1) consisting of a force-measurer, a dynamic control subsystem, and a space integrator, this derivation summary examines the consequences of adopting each of four different types of dynamic control subsystems. In each case, the point of departure is Eq. (3) of Derivation Summary 6-1, with the integration replaced by any one of four choices of dynamic control components; that is, the angular velocity of the indicated vertical with respect to the earth $\overline{W}_{(EV)i}$ is made some performance function $[PF]_{(vis)}$ of the accelerometer output:

$$\overline{W}_{(EV)i} = [PF]_{(vis)}[\overline{I}_{Vi} \times \overline{f}] \tag{1}$$

where the specific force $\overline{f}$ is given by

$$\overline{f} = \overline{I}_{Vt}g + \overline{R}_E \times p\,\overline{W}_{(EV)t} \tag{2}$$

where R_E is the earth-radius.

Case (a). Direct coupling between force-measurer and torque-producer

Here

$$[PF]_{(vis)} = S_{(vis)[f;W]} = S_{(au)[f;e]}S_{(dir)[e;i]}S_{(si)[i;W]} \tag{3}$$

where

$S_{(dir)[e,i]}$ = sensitivity of direct coupler

and $S_{(au)[f;e]}$ and $S_{(si)[i;W]}$ are as with Eq. (3) of Derivation Summary 6-1. Using the methods of Derivation Summary 6-1, the performance equation is:

$$[p + S_{(vis)[f;W]}g][(\overline{C)V}]_{(t,i)} = \overline{W}_{(EV)t} \div S_{(vis)[f;W]}R_E\, p\,\overline{W}_{(EV)t} \tag{4}$$

This equation is plotted in Fig. 6-2 as a function of the ratio of the forcing frequency w_f to the Schuler frequency w_s, where

$$w_s \equiv \sqrt{\frac{g}{R_E}}$$

In the plot, for purposes of illustration, the characteristic time is

$$CT = \frac{1}{S_{(vis)[f;W]}\,g} = 2 \text{ minutes (a typical value in practice)}$$

For this plot

$$\overline{W}_{(EV)t} = \frac{v_{gs}}{R_E}\,e^{jw_f t} \tag{5}$$

where v_{gs} is the ground speed.

Case (b). Single-integrator coupling between force-measurer and torque-producer

This case is treated in Derivation Summary 6-1.

Case (c). Integrator-and-bypass coupling

Referring to Eq. (1) and Fig. 6-4 for this case

$$[PF]_{(vis)} = S_{(int)[e;i]}\frac{1}{p} + S_{(dir)[e;i]} = S_{(int)[e;i]}\frac{1}{p}(1 + p\,T_{id}) \tag{6}$$

Derivation Summary 6-2. Dynamic control of a vertical indication loop. (Page 1 of 5)

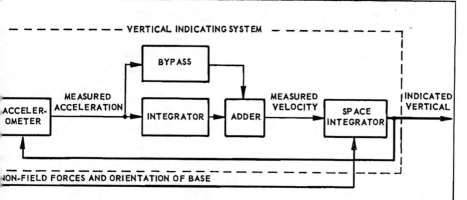

Fig. 6-4. Functional schematic of a single-axis vertical indication loop using integrator-with-bypass coupling between accelerometer unit and space integrator drive.

ere

$$T_{ld} \equiv \frac{S_{(dir)[e;i]}}{S_{(int)[e;i]}} \tag{7}$$

ing the methods of Derivation Summary 6-1, the performance equation is:

$$+ S_{(vis)[f;\dot{w}]} T_{ld}\, gp + S_{(vis)[f;\dot{w}]}\, g][\overline{(C)V}]_{(t,i)} = [(1 - S_{(vis)[f;\dot{w}]} R_E)p - S_{(vis)[f;\dot{w}]} T_{ld} R_E\, p^2]\overline{W}_{(EV)t} \tag{8}$$

the system is Schuler tuned by Eq. (13) of Derivation Summary 6-1, the performance equation be-
nes

$$\left[p^2 + T_{ld}\, \frac{g}{R_s}\, p + \frac{g}{R_s}\right][\overline{(C)V}]_{(t,i)} = -\, T_{ld}\, p^2\, \overline{W}_{(EV)t} \tag{9}$$

m which the characteristic equation has the form

$$[p^2 + 2(DR)w_n p + w_n^2][\overline{(C)V}]_{(t,i)} = 0 \tag{10}$$

ere DR the damping ratio and w_n the undamped natural frequency are

$$w_n = \sqrt{g/R_s} \tag{11}$$

$$DR = \frac{1}{2}\, T_{ld} w_n \tag{12}$$

the plot

$$\frac{g}{R_E} = 20.0\ hr^{-2}$$

, for illustrative purposes

$$DR = 0.1\ \text{(a typical value for aircraft use)}^*$$

Damping ratios up to approximately 0.3 may be used in marine systems, due to the less violent environment.

Derivation Summary 6-2. Dynamic control of a vertical indication loop. (Page 2 of 5)

F

Case (d). Integrator-with-feedback cascaded with integrator-with-bypass coupling

Figure 6-5 shows this loop; in terms of the performance function $[PF]_{(vis)}$ previously defined, here

$$[PF]_{(vis)} = \left[S_{(ldi)[e;\dot{e}]} \frac{1}{p} + S_{(dir)[e;e]} \right] \left[\frac{S_{(lgi)[e;i]}}{p + S_{(lgi)[e;i]} S_{(fb)[i;e]}} \right]$$

$$= \frac{S_{(ldi)[e;\dot{e}]}}{S_{(fb)[i;e]}} \frac{1}{p} \frac{1 + p\,T_{ld}}{1 + p\,T_{lg}} \tag{13}$$

where

$$T_{ld} = \frac{S_{(dir)[e;e]}}{S_{(ldi)[e;\dot{e}]}} \tag{14}$$

$$T_{lg} = \frac{1}{S_{(lgi)[e;i]} S_{(fb)[i;e]}} \tag{15}$$

$S_{(ldi)[e;\dot{e}]}$ = lead integrator sensitivity

$S_{(lgi)[e;i]}$ = lag integrator sensitivity

$S_{(fb)[i;e]}$ = feedback sensitivity

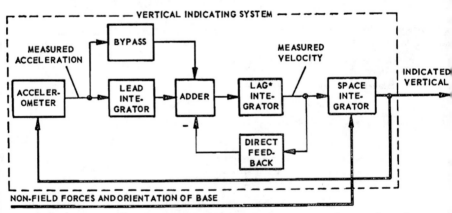

VERTICAL INDICATING SYSTEM

MEASURED ACCELERATION

BYPASS

MEASURED VELOCITY

INDICATED VERTICAL

ACCELEROMETER — LEAD INTEGRATOR — ADDER — LAG* INTEGRATOR — SPACE INTEGRATOR

DIRECT FEEDBACK

NON-FIELD FORCES AND ORIENTATION OF BASE

* This particular lag network is shown for purposes of illustration only; other forms may be used.

Fig. 6-5. Functional schematic of a single-axis vertical indication loop using integrator-with-bypass followed by lag network as coupling between accelerometer unit and space integrator drive.

Derivation Summary 6-2. Dynamic control of a vertical indication loop. (Page 3 of 5)

Carrying out the performance equation derivation gives a result that offers two choices of Schuler tuning:

$$\left[p^3 + \frac{1}{T_{1g}} p^2 + S_{(vis)[f;\dot{w}]} \frac{T_{1d}}{T_{1g}} gp + S_{(vis)[f;\dot{w}]} \frac{1}{T_{1g}} g \right] [(C)V]_{(t,1)}$$

$$= \left[\left(1 - S_{(vis)[f;\dot{w}]} \frac{T_{1d}}{T_{1g}} R_E \right) p + (1 - S_{(vis)[f;\dot{w}]} R_E) \frac{1}{T_{1g}} \right] p \, \overline{W}_{(EV)t} \qquad (16)$$

where

$$S_{(vis)[f;\dot{w}]} \equiv \frac{S_{(au)[f;e]} S_{(1d1)[e;\dot{e}]} S_{(s1)[1;W]}}{S_{(fb)[1;e]}}$$

Case (d1). The acceleration error coefficient $(1 - S_{(vis)[f;\dot{w}]} R_E)$ is zeroed for Schuler tuning, this makes Eq. (16) reduce to

$$\left[p^3 + \frac{1}{T_{1g}} p^2 + \frac{T_{1d}}{T_{1g}} \frac{g}{R_E} p + \frac{1}{T_{1g}} \frac{g}{R_E} \right] [(C)V]_{(t,1)} = \left(1 - \frac{T_{1d}}{T_{1g}} \right) p^2 \overline{W}_{(EV)t} \qquad (17)$$

Case (d2). The jerk error coefficient $(1 - S_{(vis)[f;\dot{w}]}(T_{1d}/T_{1g}) R_E)$ is zeroed for Schuler tuning, this makes Eq. (16) reduce to

$$\left[p^3 + \frac{1}{T_{1g}} p^2 + \frac{g}{R_E} p + \frac{1}{T_{1d}} \frac{g}{R_E} \right] [(C)V]_{(t,1)} = \left(\frac{1}{T_{1g}} - \frac{1}{T_{1d}} \right) p \, \overline{W}_{(EV)t} \qquad (18)$$

The characteristic equation associated with Eqs. (17) and (18) has the form

$$\left[p + \frac{1}{(CT)} \right] [p^2 + 2(DR) w_n p + w_n^2] = \left\{ p^3 + \left[2(DR) w_n + \frac{1}{(CT)} \right] p^2 \right.$$

$$\left. + \left[w_n^2 + \frac{2(DR) w_n}{(CT)} \right] p + \frac{w_n^2}{(CT)} \right\} = 0 \qquad (19)$$

Equating the individual coefficients of the left-hand side of Eqs. (17) and (18) with those of Eq. (19) permits expressing the right-hand side of the two first equations in terms of performance parameters (DR), w_n and (CT). The damping ratio is selected for best compromise between small forced error and reasonable settling time. Let w_n be the independent variable. It is desired to minimize the right-hand side of Eqs. (17) and (18);

in Eq. (17) $$\frac{d}{dw_n} \left(1 - \frac{T_{1d}}{T_{1g}} \right) = 0 \qquad (20)$$

in Eq. (18) $$\frac{d}{dw_n} \left(\frac{1}{T_{1g}} - \frac{1}{T_{1d}} \right) = 0 \qquad (21)$$

gives minimum forced error in the high-frequency regime for the selected damping ratio.

For case (d1) Eq. (20) then gives for minimum forced dynamic error

$$\left. \begin{aligned} w_n^2 &= [1 + 2(DR)] \frac{g}{R_E} \\ T &= \frac{1}{w_n} \end{aligned} \right\} \qquad (22)$$

Derivation Summary 6-2. Dynamic control of a vertical indication loop. (Page 4 of 5) and for case (d2) Eq. (21) gives similarly

$$w_n^2 = [1 - (DR)^2] \frac{g}{R_E} \Bigg\} \qquad (23)$$

$$T = \frac{(DR)}{2w_n}$$

in this case

$$\sqrt{1 - (DR)^2 + (DR)^4} \longrightarrow 1 - \frac{1}{2}(DR)^2 + \cdots$$

Both Eqs. (22) and (23) have sufficiently constant values near the optimum to allow some variation in T_{1d} and T_{1g} without altering performance appreciably.

Derivation Summary 6-2. Dynamic control of a vertical indication loop. (Page 5 of 5)

high-frequency regime, due to the long natural period implied by Schuler tuning and the fact that significant accelerations are associated only with maneuvers having periods of a few minutes. This quality is displayed in the graph, Fig. 6-2.

Note that ground speed in Fig. 6-2 means specifically that particular component of ground speed which could be expected to affect the single-axis vertical indication loop under consideration. Thus, in a system indicating the vertical in geographic coordinates, the loop associated with rotations about a northerly axis would be affected by the longitude rate of the vehicle, or the east–west component of its ground speed, with a similar relationship holding between the loop rotating about an easterly axis and the latitude rate or the north-south component of ground speed of the vehicle.

The dynamic performance of these third-order systems can be described completely in terms of the damping ratio, the undamped natural frequency of the quadratic term, and the characteristic time of the first-order term. The numerical values of these three quantities determine the values of component sensitivities. These three parameters are universally applicable in the description of linear systems of this general nature. In one design method, for example, the numerical values are assigned according to the following procedures:

1. The damping ratio has, for minimum forced error, an optimum value of zero; but the resulting undamped system would be objectionable for the reasons already given. The chosen damping ratio is therefore a compromise between acceptably small forced

error and a reasonable solution time.* Since the damping ratio is small (experience shows value of 0.1 to 0.3 to be best) the undamped natural period of the quadratic factor may be assumed to be close to the Schuler period.

2. The undamped natural frequency for the quadratic factor is then chosen to minimize the forced dynamic error in the performance equation for either the jerk- or acceleration-tuned systems. The natural frequency thus found is a function of the chosen damping ratio. Proper values are given in Derivation Summary 6-2.

3. Given the damping ratio and the undamped resonant frequency, the characteristic time of the first-order factor is automatically determined by the Schuler-tuning condition.

Damping and phase control

Frictional damping in mechanics implies the dissipation of energy of the system to the environment in order to achieve a change of equilibrium state. In contrast, damping in control systems of the type discussed in this section means the total process of the splitting of the signal at some point in the loop, the processing of the two resulting signals so that one leads or lags the other, and their recombination (see the lead integrator and direct channel in Fig. 6-4). The required energy change takes place in the servo motor. The method, suitably applied, will create a tendency on the part of the system to seek the mean output, if the output is oscillating about a mean value. Thus damping control is conveniently carried out at a signal rather than a power level and involves both oscillatory energy transfer from system to environment and the control of the phase of one portion of the signal in the loop with respect to another portion. Power changes take place in the power-producing component, namely the servo motor and power supplies.

Phase control produces damping without forced error when the signal which is split is purely a signal to be nulled. In the vertical indicator, where the accelerometer output is approximately proportional to a gravity component plus acceleration, only the gravity term is a nulled signal, the acceleration term producing the inherent tracking aid when the system is Schuler-tuned. Any attempt to damp the system, however, affects the acceleration term also. These two terms are not measurably separable; that is, the effects of a gravity component due to accelerometer tilt and of linear acceleration of the accelerometer are seen by

---

* Solution time is defined for present purposes as the time required for a linear system to achieve ninety-five per cent of the output change associated with a given step-input change

the system in the same way. The result of the processing of the acceleration term by the damping elements is that extra signals are sent to the integrating drive over and above the signals required for correct settling in of the vertical indicator. These signals create the forced errors accompanying damping.

The frequency spectrum of the tangential acceleration of the vehicle over the surface of the earth will be a function of vehicle maneuvers. If they are such that the forcing frequency is high compared to the reciprocal of the lead and lag times (which are only slightly different values if the system is appropriately damped) the jerk-tuned system is most suitable. Similarly, relatively low-frequency forcing functions suggest the use of an acceleration-tuned system.

Referring again to Fig. 6-2, it should be noted that, were the damping sufficiently reduced in either system, the system would approach an equivalent Schuler pendulum with a natural frequency corresponding to a unity frequency ratio, with the Schuler frequency as the reference frequency. In the case of the two third-order systems, the frequency ratio for maximum amplitude ratio is higher than unity for acceleration-error elimination and lower than unity for jerk-error elimination; the departure of the frequency ratio from unity is determined in both cases by the damping ratio of the quadratic factor. The relative heights of the peaks in the curve are also determined by the damping ratio. The choice between the two response functions can then be based on whether it is desirable, relatively speaking, to suppress low frequencies or high frequencies; i.e., whether the expected forcing inputs will be primarily of a high- or low-frequency character, relative to the Schuler period.

Summary of the uses of damping

The vertical indicating system described by Eq.(19) in Derivation Summary 6-1 is undamped. Given an initial displacement error, it oscillates continuously at constant amplitude about the vertical. An undamped Schuler-tuned vertical indicator is subject to continuous oscillation with a strong Fourier-component period of about 84 minutes, the Schuler period, due primarily to initial-condition errors or to instrument imperfections. An undamped system might be practical under the following conditions:

1. The time of operation is sufficiently short, i.e., of the order of one

or two natural periods, so that damping could not have time to become effective during the operating interval.

2. The initial conditions are set into the system with sufficient precision (a condition difficult to realize in practice). This means that the amplitude of oscillation will not exceed the allowable error in the indication of the vertical. Also, component errors are not appreciable.

While in operation, the system may acquire errors larger than the initial uncaging errors. This is because component behavior may change unpredictably in time; in general, the longer the operating time, the greater the probability of a change in system parameters because of a change in component sensitivity or linearity. Either gyro drift or integrator drift would be a case in point, but it must not be assumed that such drift is a strictly linear function of the elapsed time of operation.

Damping has the effect of limiting the oscillation of the system so that the instantaneous computed values of vehicle position approach average levels instead of oscillating continuously. Regarded as a device which receives information on the force on the accelerometers and transforms these data into position information, the system is a channel with a frequency response governed by the presence and nature of the damping used. Frequency response, damping, and the time required for averaging are related as follows:

1. Insofar as damping suppresses frequencies that are high relative to the system's natural time parameters, it delays the response of the system to input changes. This effect is important in determining the system's solution time, both when the system is initially uncaged and when it suffers transient disturbances while the vehicle carrying the system is in motion.

2. The delay in achieving a solution is operative at other times also, in that a damped system responds to values of the input averaged over a time of the order of the solution time, rather than to instantaneous input values. The result is manifested as an output quantity that depends on the frequency distribution of the input.

The desirable aspect of damping is the averaging of system output oscillation, and the undesirable aspect is the forced dynamic error. An unavoidable compromise between adequate smoothing, short solution time, and small forced dynamic errors confronts the designer of any practical system.

CHAPTER 7

GYROS AND ACCELEROMETERS

SINCE an inertial guidance system is absolutely dependent on the performance of its gyros and accelerometers, these components must be understood in terms of their operation as instruments if the practical qualities of inertial guidance are to be made clear. Although, as the historical development in Chapter 2 shows, both gyros and accelerometers have had a long and useful past prior to the requirement for inertial guidance, their adaptation to inertial guidance has removed them a long way from the artificial horizon and the gyrocompass. An understanding of gyros and accelerometers as they are used in inertial guidance is therefore best obtained through an examination of the roles they play in modern guidance systems. This approach[18] abandons classical theory for certain instrumental simplifications, and has the virtue of emphasizing function without restricting validity. The functions of accelerometers and gyros will be considered separately. The first such function to be considered concerns the application of gyros. It is the inertial-space-referred integrating drive system.

Gyros as space-stabilization components

Any mechanism capable of indicating an orientation that remains unchanging with respect to the 'fixed stars' must depend upon the inertial properties of matter. It is convenient to utilize this property as it is associated with a spinning rotor. The spin axis of this rotor will precess (that is, change its orientation with respect to inertial space) at a rate proportional to the magnitude of the applied torque; and if this torque could be reduced to zero, the rotor spin axis would hold its direction perfectly—that is, free of drift—with respect to inertial space, which for navigation purposes is identical with celestial space. In practice, means for supporting a spinning rotor are difficult to realize without exerting unwanted torques on the rotor. Experience has shown that the uncertainty torques imposed in 'brute force' stabilization by mechanical systems driven directly from the rotor are intolerably great for inertial-system applications. The universally accepted remedy for this difficulty is to use servomechanism techniques for driving the mechanical members that support the spinning rotor. Any level of output torque can then be controlled by the spin-axis direction without imposing any significant reaction on the rotor, and the gyroscopic change in angular momentum of a spinning body can be freed of externally-caused disturbances.

The elimination of outside interfering-torque effects by the use of servo-drive arrangements places the responsibility for drift uncertainties on the designers of the gyro units. These units have two related functions to perform as components of inertial-space reference systems. First, when they are forcibly displaced from preset reference orientations, ⌐ they must generate output signals that represent these deviations, so that these signals (amplified) may be used to torque the gyros back to their reference orientations. Second, they must change these reference orientations in response to command-signal inputs, when this is required. Gyro-unit design is centered around the problem of realizing these characteristics.[19]

Gyroscopic theory

Gyroscopic theory deals with the directional aspects of the mechanics of rotating bodies. For the description of gyroscopic instruments, the general theory of rotating bodies, based on Newton's laws of motion applied to rotation, may be greatly simplified. This simplification is made possible by the fact that, for gyroscopic-instrument applications, a rotor must be carefully balanced about its axis of symmetry and be driven with a constant angular velocity of spin relative to its mounting. In practice, the spin is several orders of magnitude greater than the inertially-referred angular velocity of the instrument itself. This fact makes it easy to deal with gyroscopic effects in terms of simple vectors that represent rotational quantities.

Figure 7-1 is a summary of vector conventions for rotational quantities. Derivation Summary 7-1 summarizes the pertinent definitions, and gives a derivation of the basic performance equation, for the gyroscopic element. It is to be noted that the gyroscopic element is most effectively and completely represented by a 'disembodied' angular momentum spin vector. Figure 7-2 is a line-schematic diagram for a gimballed two-degree-of-freedom gyro mechanism illustrating the vector quantities associated with precession. It is apparent that if the applied torques from external sources and the supporting arrangement are zero, the angular-momentum vector will have zero angular velocity with respect to inertial space, and the spin axis fixed to the rotor-carrying gimbal will serve as an inertial-reference direction. The orientation of this reference direction can be changed at will with respect to inertial space by applying proper torque components—commands—to the gimbal.

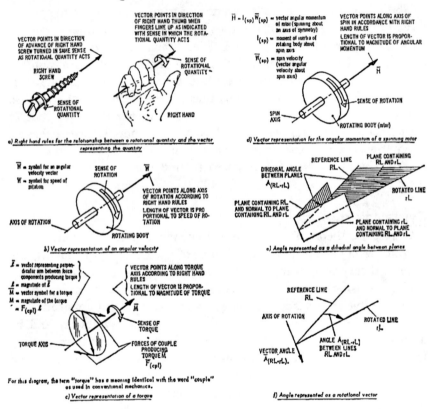

Fig. 7-1. Vector representation of rotational quantities.

Figure 7-3 is a line-schematic diagram showing the essential features of the single-degree-of-freedom gyro mechanism with viscous-damper integration, the *integrating gyro.* [20, 21, 22, 23] In this arrangement, the rotor-carrying gimbal is directly pivoted with respect to the structure that serves as the case for attaching the gyro unit to the member whose orientation with respect to inertial space is to be indicated. For convenience in discussions, three mutually perpendicular axes fixed to the

The objective of this derivation is to show how the equation of motion of a gyroscopic element follows from a simple vector formulation of the problem.

$\bar{H}_{(ge)}$ = angular momentum vector of gyroscopic element

$$= \bar{H}_{(sp)} + \bar{H}_{(n\text{-}sp)}$$

where

$H_{(sp)}$ = spin angular momentum vector of rotor
$$= I_{(sp)} W_{(sp)}$$

$\bar{H}_{(n\text{-}sp)}$ = non-spin angular momentum vector of gyroscopic element

$I_{(sp)}$ = spin moment of inertia of rotor

$\bar{W}_{(sp)}$ = spin angular velocity vector of rotor

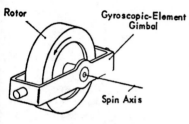

Rotor

Gyroscopic-Element Gimbal

Spin Axis

Gyroscopic Element

y definition, a practical gyroscopic element is a physical system with the following properties:

1. The rotor spins about an axis of symmetry.
2. The rotor spins at a constant speed, i.e., $W_{(sp)}$ = constant.
3. Spin angular momentum is much greater than non-spin momentum.

a) *Vector representation of a gyroscopic element*

By Newton's law for rotation,

$$\left[\frac{d\bar{H}_{(ge)}}{dt}\right]_I = \bar{M}_{(ge)(app)} \tag{1}$$

e.,

{ time rate of change of angular momentum of gyroscopic element relative to inertial space } = {torque applied to gyroscopic element}

y the equation of Coriolis (see Chap. 7 of "Vector Analysis" by J. G. Coffin)

$$\left[\frac{d\bar{X}}{dt}\right]_r = \left[\frac{d\bar{X}}{dt}\right]_m + \bar{W}_{(rm)} \times \bar{X} \tag{2}$$

here

$\bar{X}$ = any vector

$[d\bar{X}/dt]_r$ = time rate of change of $\bar{X}$ relative to space r

$[d\bar{X}/dt]_m$ = time rate of change of $\bar{X}$ relative to space m

$\bar{W}_{(rm)}$ = angular velocity of space m relative to space r

th inertial space as space r and the gyroscopic element gimbal as space m, Eq. (2) applied to Eq. (1) ves

$$\left[\frac{d\bar{H}_{(ge)}}{dt}\right]_I = \left[\frac{d\bar{H}_{(ge)}}{dt}\right]_{(ge)} + \bar{W}_{[I(ge)]} \times \bar{H}_{(ge)} = \bar{M}_{(ge)(app)} \tag{3}$$

parating $H_{(ge)}$ into its spin and non-spin components gives

$$\left[\frac{d\bar{H}_{(sp)}}{dt}\right]_{(ge)} + \left[\frac{d\bar{H}_{(n\text{-}sp)}}{dt}\right]_{(ge)} + \bar{W}_{[I(ge)]} \times \bar{H}_{(sp)} + \bar{W}_{[I(ge)]} \times \bar{H}_{(n\text{-}sp)} = \bar{M}_{(ge)(app)} \tag{4}$$

erivation Summary 7-1. Vector representation and basic performance equation for the gyroscopic element.
(Page 1 of 2)

but, by the definition of a practical gyroscopic element,

$$\left[\frac{d\overline{H}_{(sp)}}{dt}\right]_{(ge)} = 0 \qquad \text{since} \qquad |\overline{W}_{(sp)}| = \text{constant}$$

and

$$\overline{H}_{(sp)} >> \overline{H}_{(n-sp)}$$

Therefore,

$$\left[\frac{d\overline{H}_{(n-sp)}}{dt}\right]_{(ge)} + \overline{W}_{[I(ge)]} \times \overline{H}_{(sp)} = \overline{M}_{(ge)(app)} \qquad (5)$$

is the basic law of motion for a practical gyroscopic element. The term $[dH_{(n-sp)}/dt]_{(ge)}$ represents the characteristic dynamics of the gyroscopic element giving rise to nutation in a two-degree-of-freedom unit and to the characteristic time or natural period in a single-degree-of-freedom unit. In normal steady-state operation, this term is negligible relative to the spin momentum precession. Hence,

$$\overline{W}_{[I(ge)]} \times \overline{H}_{(sp)} = \overline{M}_{(ge)(app)} \qquad (6)$$

becomes the steady-state expression. Note that in Eq. (6) the gyroscopic element is completely represented by a "disembodied" angular-momentum vector. It, and it alone, is the basic parameter that represents a practical gyroscopic element.

b) *Performance equation*

Derivation Summary 7-1. Vector representation and basic performance equation for the gyroscopic element
(Page 2 of 2)

case are identified. The output axis (symbol OA) is identical with the axis about which the gimbal is pivoted with respect to the case. The spin reference axis (symbol SRA) is identical with the direction of the spin axis when the gimbal-output-angle indicator is at zero. The input axis (symbol IA) is fixed to the case so that it completes a right-handed set of orthogonal axes.

In operation, a torque applied to the case about the input axis causes the spin axis to precess about the output axis so that it turns toward the input axis. This gimbal angular velocity about the output axis sets up velocity gradients in the fluid that fills the clearance volume of the gimbal with respect to the case. For situations in which steady-state dynamic conditions exist, so that inertia-reaction effects are not significant, the angular velocity of the gimbal is constant and the viscous-damping torque has a magnitude equal to the output torque from the gyroscopic element. A derivation of the equations that express this fact is given in Derivation Summary 7-2.

From the standpoint of usefulness for practical applications, the essential result is that, over any given time interval during which the gimbal is free and the gimbal angle (the angle measured from the spin reference axis to the spin axis) remains small, the integral of the angular velocity of the gimbal (the angular displacement) with respect to the case is proportional to the angular displacement of the case with respect to inertial space about the input axis. It is important to note that there is no preferred natural orientation of the case from which the motion of the case is started with respect to inertial space. The reference

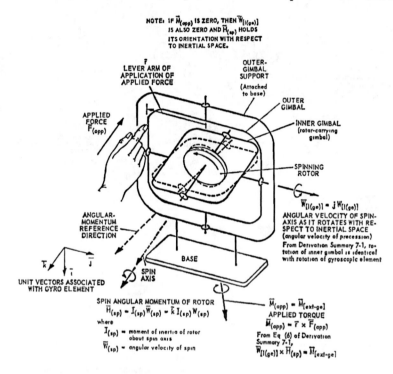

Fig. 7-2. Line-schematic diagram for a two-degree-of-freedom gyro mechanism, illustrating the vector quantities associated with precession.

orientation, an *initial condition*, is established by the physical mechanism of the gyro unit and its orientation at some instant that is taken as zero for integration of angular velocity. Usually it is convenient to take the reference orientation as the position of the case at an instant when the spin axis is aligned with the spin reference axis, that is, when the gimbal angle is zero.

In any practical case, the gimbal output angle is never allowed to become greater than a few seconds of arc, so it is valid to assume that the direction of the angular-momentum vector is *always* along the spin reference axis.

Gyro-unit applications

Inaccuracy levels permitted by the performance requirements of inertial systems are so low that calibrations, that is, stable and accurately known input-to-output relationships, are difficult or impossible to

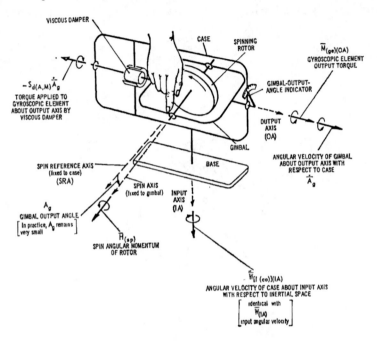

The basic performance equation for a single-degree-of freedom gyro unit with a viscous damper can be derived as follows

$$S_{d(\dot{A},M)}\dot{\vec{A}}_g = \overline{W}_{(IA)} \times \overline{H}_{(sp)}$$

This means that as long as $\overline{H}_{(sp)}$ remains essentially perpendicular to the input axis, IA, the relationship between angular velocities is

$$\dot{A}_g = \frac{H_{(sp)}}{S_{d(\dot{A},M)}} W_{(IA)}$$

so that

$$\boxed{A_g = \int_0^t \dot{A}_g\, dt = \frac{H_{(sp)}}{S_{d(\dot{A},M)}} \int_0^t W_{(IA)}\, dt}$$

If both angular displacements are zero at t = 0

Note: The preceding performance equation is based on the assumption that inertia-reaction effects due to angular accelerations about the output axis are negligible and that the gimbal output angle remains small.

Fig. 7-3. Line-schematic diagram for a single-degree-of-freedom gyro mechanism with viscous damping, illustrating vector quantities associated with operation.

establish and maintain over wide ranges of operation. An alternate and preferable mode of operation is *nulling*, in which the position of the null must be very accurately held but in which the sensing units only need to indicate the directions and approximate magnitudes of input

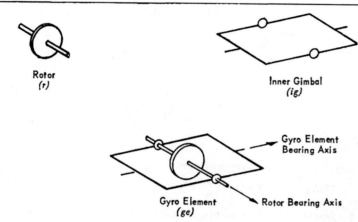

Rotor
(r)

Inner Gimbal
(ig)

Gyro Element
Bearing Axis

Gyro Element
(ge)

Rotor Bearing Axis

The gyro element is the combination of rotor and inner gimbal.

The Two-Degree-of-Freedom Gyro

From Eq. (5) of Derivation Summary 7-1,

$$[\dot{\overline{H}}_{(ns)}]_{(ge)} + \overline{W}_{[I(ge)]} \times \overline{H}_{(sp)} = \overline{M}_{[ext-ge]} \tag{1}$$

which is the vector performance equation for a practical gyro element.

To apply this equation to a two-degree-of-freedom gyro unit, choose unit vectors, $\overline{\imath}, \overline{\jmath}, \overline{k}$ for the (ge)-frame as shown in Fig. 7-2, where:

$\overline{k}$ is along the spin axis in the same direction as $\overline{H}_{(sp)}$

$\overline{\jmath}$ is along the gyro element bearing axis

$\overline{\imath}$ completes a right-handed triad

$[\ ^{\cdot}\ ] = [d/dt]$

$$\overline{H}_{(sp)} = \overline{k}H_{(sp)} = \overline{k}I_{(sp)}\overline{W}_{(sp)}$$

$$\overline{W}_{[I(ge)]} = \overline{\imath}W_{[I(ge)]x} + \overline{\jmath}W_{[I(ge)]y} + \overline{k}W_{[I(ge)]z} \tag{2}$$

$$\overline{H}_{(ns)} = \overline{\imath}I_x W_{[I(ge)]x} + \overline{\jmath}I_y W_{[I(ge)]y} + \overline{k}I_z W_{[I(ge)]z}$$

where

$W_{[I(ge)]z}$ does not include the spin angular velocity $W_{(sp)}$.

Substitute Eq. (2) into Eq. (1) to obtain the component equations of motion of the gyro element, namely, the $\overline{\imath}$ and $\overline{\jmath}$ components:

$$I_x \dot{W}_{[I(ge)]x} + H_{(sp)} W_{[I(ge)]y} = M_{[ext-ge]x}$$

$$I_y \dot{W}_{[I(ge)]y} - H_{(sp)} W_{[I(ge)]x} = M_{[ext-ge]y} \tag{3}$$

Derivation Summary 7-2. Equations of motion of gyroscopic units. (Page 1 of 4)

(The equation for the $\bar{k}$ component is irrelevant in describing the equation of a practical gyroscopic unit.) The solution of Eqs. (3) for $W_{[I(ge)]x}$ and $W_{[I(ge)]y}$ may be written in the form

$$\left[\frac{p^2}{W_{nu}^2} + 1\right] W_{[I(ge)]x} = -\frac{M_y}{H_{(sp)}} + \frac{pM_x}{I_x W_{nu}^2}$$

$$\left[\frac{p^2}{W_{nu}^2} + 1\right] W_{[I(ge)]y} = \frac{M_x}{H_{(sp)}} + \frac{pM_y}{I_y W_{nu}^2}$$

(4)

where

$$p \equiv d/dt$$

$W_{nu}^2 = H_{(sp)}^2/I_x I_y = $ square of the nutation frequency

Since I_x, I_y, I_z and $I_{(sp)}$ are of the same order of magnitude, the nutation frequency, W_{nu}, is approximately equal to the spin angular velocity.

If the nutation is damped (by means that must be inertial, but that for simplicity are not shown) or if the torques M_x and M_y contain no significant amplitude components near the frequency W_{nu}, then the gyro-element equations (4) have the solutions

$$W_{[I(ge)]x} = -\frac{M_y}{H_{(sp)}}$$

$$W_{[I(ge)]y} = \frac{M_x}{H_{(sp)}}$$

(5)

These are the solutions that would have been directly obtained from Eq. (6) of Derivation Summary 7-1, in which the gyro unit is represented solely by its "disembodied" angular momentum of spin.

II. The Single-Degree-of-Freedom Gyro

The single-degree-of-freedom gyro consists of a gyro element that is free to rotate <u>with respect to the case</u> only about the gyro-element bearing axis.

The appropriate coordinate axes in this case are the input, output, and spin reference axes, which are fixed to the case, as shown in Fig. 7-3, and may be considered as the $\bar{\imath}$, $\bar{\jmath}$, and $\bar{k}$ axes of Eqs. (2).

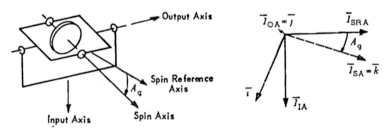

Let the components of the angular velocity of the case with respect to inertial space be denoted as follows:

$$W_{[I(ca)](IA)} \equiv W_{(IA)} \quad ; \quad W_{[I(ca)](OA)} \equiv W_{(OA)} \quad ; \quad W_{[I(ca)](SRA)} \equiv W_{(SRA)}$$

Derivation Summary 7-2. Equations of motion of gyroscopic units. (Page 2 of 4)

Then

$$W_{[I(ge)]x} = W_{(IA)} \cos A_g - W_{(SRA)} \sin A_g$$

$$W_{[I(ge)]y} = W_{(OA)} + \dot{A}_g \qquad (6)$$

$$W_{[I(ge)]z} = W_{(SRA)} \cos A_g + W_{(IA)} \sin A_g$$

$A_g = A_{[ca\text{-}ge]}$

= angle of rotation (precession) of gyro element relative to the gyro-unit case

substitute Eqs. (6) into Eqs. (2) and (1) to obtain for the $\bar{j}$ (output axis) component, the only component of interest in a practical single-degree-of-freedom gyro unit:

$$I_g (\dot{W}_{(OA)} + \ddot{A}_g) - H_{(sp)}(W_{(IA)} \cos A_g - W_{(SRA)} \sin A_g) = M_{(ext\text{-}ge)y} = M_{(OA)} \qquad (7)$$

where

$I_g = I_y$ = moment of inertia of gyro element about the output axis

In the integrating gyro (sometimes called a rate integrating gyro), calibrated torques are applied to the gyro element by a damper as well as by a torque generator, which produces a torque proportional to its input (command) current. Therefore,

$$M_{(OA)} = -S_{g(\dot{A},M)} \dot{A}_g - S_{(tg)(i,M)} i_{(cmd)} + (U)M_g \qquad (8)$$

where

$i_{(cmd)}$ = command current = input current to torque generator

$(U)M_g$ = torque uncertainty about the output axis

The gyro equation is, by substituting Eq. (8) into Eq. (7) and rearranging terms,

$$I_g \ddot{A}_g + S_{g(\dot{A},M)} \dot{A}_g = H_{(sp)}(W_{(IA)} \cos A_g - W_{(SRA)} \sin A_g) - S_{(tg)(i,M)} i_{(cmd)} + (U)M_g - I_g \dot{W}_{(OA)} \qquad (9)$$

The integrating gyro is used only as an element of a closed-loop system that maintains A_g small so that $\cos A_g \cong 1$ and $\sin A_g \cong A_g$, giving for Eq. (9)

$$[(CT)_g p + 1] p A_g = \frac{H_{(sp)}}{S_{g(\dot{A},M)}} [W_{(IA)} - W_{(cmd)} + (U)W_g] - (CT)_g p W_{(OA)} \qquad (10)$$

where

$(CT)_g = I_g/S_{g(\dot{A},M)}$ = characteristic time of gyro unit

$W_{(cmd)} = S_{(tg)(i,M)} i_{(cmd)}/H_{(sp)}$ = command angular velocity

$(U)W_g = (U)M_g/H_{(sp)}$ = drift uncertainty due to torque uncertainty

The interaxis coupling term $A_g W_{(SRA)}$ has been neglected, because of the small value of A_g in practical operation.

Precision integrating gyros all use fluids to support the gyro element, in order to reduce friction torques that would produce unacceptably large gimbal angle uncertainty. Two types of fluid support have been employed. In the first, the gyro element floats in a liquid whose density is very close to being equal to the average density of the gyro element. The liquids used may have large or small viscosity. In the second type, pressurized fluid flow, either compressible or incompressible, is used to prevent contact between the gyro element and the case.

The integrating gyros may be separated into three classes on the basis of the gyro-element support: 1) highly viscous liquid, 2) lightly viscous liquid, and 3) air bearing (compressible fluid with pressure

Derivation Summary 7-2. Equations of motion of gyroscopic units. (Page 3 of 4)

G

drop). Strictly speaking, only type (1) is an integrating gyro in normal operation. Characteristics of the three types are summarized in the following table.

	$H_{(sp)}/S_{g(\dot{A},M)}$	$I_g/S_{g(\dot{A},M)}$	$I_g/H_{(sp)}$	Typical $H_{(sp)}$
Highly viscous fluid support	1	10^{-3} sec	10^{-3} sec	10^6 gm-cm^2/sec
Lightly viscous fluid support	10^2	10^{-1}	10^{-3}	10^6
Air bearing	10^5	10^2	10^{-3}	10^7

III. Reaction Torques

The reaction torques that the gyro element applies to the case about the input and output axes may be important in design considerations, since these torques must eventually act on the structure that supports the case. The torques may be evaluated by use of Eqs. (3) substituted into the negative of Eq. (6) of Derivation Summary 7-1, and resolution from gyro element axes into case axes.

$$M_{[ge-ca](IA)} = -M_{(IA)} = -I_x \dot{W}_{(IA)} - H_{(sp)}(W_{(OA)} + \dot{A}_g)$$

$$M_{[ge-ca](OA)} = -M_{(OA)} = -M_{(OA)} + (U)M_g$$

(11)

In the derivation of Eqs. (11), $\cos A_g \cong 1$, $\sin A_g \cong A_g$ and all products of gimbal angle and gimbal rate with case angular velocities were neglected.

Derivation Summary 7-2. Equations of motion of gyroscopic units. (Page 4 of 4)

deviations from reference conditions. These input-deviation indications are used as command signals for servo-type feedback loops that act to drive the input sensor toward its position for null output. In arrangements of this kind, the input receiver acts as the error-sensing means that is an essential component of any servo system. In order to describe the functions of gyro units and specific-force receivers as components of inertial systems, Figs. 7-4 and 7-5 give illustrative pictorial-schematic diagrams of a single-axis inertial-space stabilization and integration system and a specific-force integrating receiver, respectively.

In Fig. 7-4, the gyro unit is rigidly attached to a controlled member which, for illustrative purposes, is shown as servodriven about a single axis. The input axis of the gyro unit is aligned with the controlled-member axis, so that the output axis and the spin reference axis lie in the plane normal to the servodrive axis. The signal-generator output of the gyro unit is connected through slip rings to the input of the electronic power control unit for the servodrive motor. When the gimbal angle is zero, the spin axis is aligned with the spin reference axis, the signal-generator output is at its null (minimum) level, and the gyro-unit output axis establishes the reference orientation for the controlled member. When the direction of the gyro-unit input axis is nonrotating with respect to inertial space and the gyro-rotor gimbal is free from all applied torques, except those stemming from power leads, friction, and the like, the arrangement of Fig. 7-4 gives single-axis geometrical stabilization with respect to inertial space.

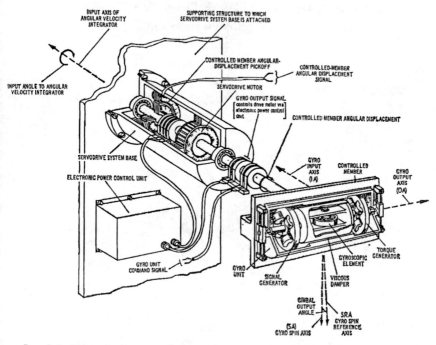

Fig. 7-4. Pictorial-schematic diagram of a single-degree-of-freedom servodriven inertial reference angular velocity integrator

Starting with the controlled member in its reference position, the direction of the controlled-member axis may be rotated in any possible way with respect to inertial space and the gyro-unit output signal will remain at its null level as long as the controlled member is not rotated about the gyro-unit input axis away from its reference orientation, although the reference orientation may itself rotate with respect to inertial space. If the controlled member does deviate from the reference orientation for any reason, the gyro rotor and gimbal rotate with respect to the case, and the output signal changes from its null level. The slip rings and electrical connections transfer this signal change to the electronic power control unit, which in turn changes the input power to the servodrive motor in such a way that the controlled member is turned back toward the reference orientation. This action continues during any rotations of the base about the gyro-unit input axis, so that the controlled member *hunts* about the reference orientation with very small angular deviations. This entire process is called base-motion isolation or geometrical stabilization. The performance equation for a single-axis base-motion isolation system is detailed in Derivation Summary 7-3. The functional diagram for such a system is shown in Fig. 7-6.

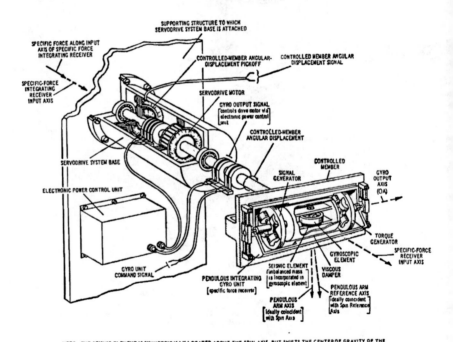

NOTE   THE SEISMIC ELEMENT IS SYMMETRICALLY LOCATED ABOUT THE SPIN AXIS BUT SHIFTS THE CENTER OF GRAVITY OF THE GYROSCOPIC ELEMENT ALONG THE SPIN AXIS AWAY FROM THE OUTPUT AXIS

Fig. 7-5. Pictorial-schematic diagram for a single-degree-of-freedom specific-force integrating receiver based on the single-degree-of-freedom pendulous integrating gyro unit and a single-axis servodriven controlled member.

In practice, three single-degree-of-freedom gyro units are mounted so that their input axes are mutually at right angles on a controlled member. The controlled member has three degrees of angular freedom with respect to its base, required to give complete geometrical stabilization. With this arrangement, each of the three gyro units supplies deviation signals about a controlled-member-fixed direction that changes its orientation with respect to the servodrive-motor axes, so that the

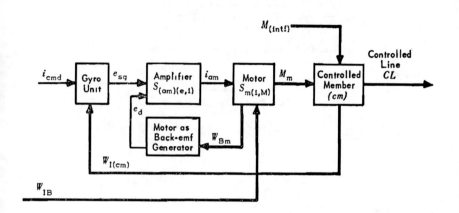

Functional diagram of a single-axis space integrator.

The above figure should be compared with Fig. 7-6.

$$I_{(cm)}P W_{I(cm)} = M_m + Ip W_{IB} + M_{(intf)}$$

$$M_m = S_{m(i,M)} t_{am}$$

$$t_{am} = S_{(am)(e,i)}(e_{(sq)} - e_d) \qquad (1)$$

$$e_d = S_{d(W,e)} W_{Bm}*$$

$$W_{Bm} = W_{B(cm)} = W_{I(cm)} - W_{IB}$$

Combining these equations and collecting terms gives

$$[I_{(cm)}P + S_{S[W,M]}] W_{I(cm)} = S_{m(i,M)} S_{(am)(e,i)} e_{(sq)} + S_{S[W,M]} W_{IB} + M_{(intf)} \qquad (2)$$

where

$$S_{S[W,M]} \equiv S_{m(i,M)} S_{(am)(e,i)} S_{d(W,e)}$$

This is the performance equation of the **drive system**. The drive system is represented below in a simplified functional diagram.

* The damping here represents only that due to the back e.m.f. of the direct-acting torque motor. It is realized that such damping is inadequate and that phase-shifting of the gyro output signal would be used in practice. However, the above is used merely to keep the problem simple, so that servo problems would not mask the basic space-integrator, operation.

Derivation Summary 7-3. Single-axis space integrator using a single-degree-of-freedom integrating gyro.
(Page 1 of 2)

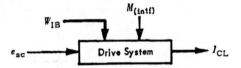

Simplified functional diagram of drive system.

The signal comparator voltage is

$$e_{(sg)} = S_{(sg)(A,e)} A_g \qquad (3)$$

From Eq. (10) of Derivation Summary 7-2 and Eq. (3), Eq. (2) becomes

$$\left\{ [(CT)_q p + 1] \left[\frac{p^2}{W_{ns}^2} + \frac{2\zeta_a p}{W_{ns}} \right] + 1 \right\} W_{1(cm)} = S_{(s1)(1,W)} i_{(cmd)} - (U)W_q + \frac{l_q}{H_{(sp)}} pW_{(OA)}$$

$$+ [(CT)_q p + 1] \left\{ \frac{2\zeta_a p}{W_{ns}} W_{1B} + \frac{pM_{(intf)}}{S_{(s1)(A,M)}} \right\} \quad (4)$$

where

$$S_{(s1)(1,W)} \equiv S_{(tg)(1,M)}/H_{(sp)}$$

$$S_{(s1)(A,M)} \equiv S_{(sg)(A,e)} S_{(cm)(e,1)} S_{m(1,M)} H_{(sp)}/S_g(\dot{A},M)$$

$$W_{ns}^2 \equiv S_{s(A,M)}/l_{(cm)}$$

$$2\zeta_s/W_{ns} \equiv S_{s(W,M)}/l_{(cm)}$$

Equation (4) is the performance equation for a single-axis space integrator with an integrating gyro as the space sensor.

Derivation Summary 7-3. Single-axis space integrator using a single-degree-of-freedom integrating gyro.
(Page 2 of 2)

deviation signals must be distributed by a system of resolvers to insure action by the proper motors. This is a low-accuracy resolution that serves only to maintain reasonably constant servo-loop gains. The action of each gyro protects the other two from rotations about axes other than their own input axes, so that it is a simple matter to achieve stabilization in the accuracy region of one second of arc. This geometrical filtering action places the engineering-design burden on the minimizing of drift rates in the gyro units, rather than in the servo.

For the purposes of controlling flight vehicles, three single-degree-of-freedom gyros are often mounted rigidly to a vehicle structure. They generate signals that represent angular deviations from a reference orientation of the vehicle, which is then indeed the controlled member. These signals are command inputs for the vehicle orientational control system. The actual vehicle orientation hunts about the vehicle reference orientation with angular deviations that depend on the quality of the vehicle control system, which here is a servodrive in a vehicle stabilization loop.

Some proposals and attempts have been made to base high-quality inertial guidance systems on single-degree-of-freedom gyros mounted rigidly to vehicle structures. A peculiarity of the arrangement is that the gyros must be capable of handling, simultaneously, vehicle roll, pitch, and yaw components in the region of one radian per second and inertial-guidance angular velocities of less than 10^{-8} radian per second. Accurate

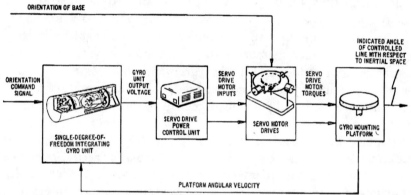

Fig. 7-6. Single-degree-of-freedom integrating gyro unit used in a space integrator.

resolutions and computations are required over this range of magnitudes, with gyro-unit calibrations accurate over angles that are much greater than the few seconds of arc that are involved when geometrically-stabilized packages are used. Various configurations of components are possible in systems based on vehicle-structure-mounted gyro units and specific-force receivers. All of these arrangements impose these calibration and computation requirements on components, requirements that are much more severe than those on a separately-stabilized inertial package.

The full usefulness of the servodriven controlled member–gyro unit combination appears when the torque generator in the gyro unit of Fig. 7-4 receives a command signal from some external source. The corresponding torque-generator output torque is applied to the gimbal about the output axis of the gyro unit so that the spin axis turns away from the spin reference axis. This deviation causes the signal-generator output to change from its null level so that the servodrive motor rotates the controlled member at some finite angular velocity. The gyro rotor

about the gyro's IA

responds to this angular velocity by applying its output torque to the gimbal in the direction that tends to return the spin axis to alignment with the spin reference axis. With suitable power-control-system design, equilibrium exists when this alignment is reached and the output signal is at its null level. This means that the angular velocity of the controlled member with respect to inertial space about the gyro input axis is directly proportional to the torque-generator output torque if the angular momentum of the rotor is constant. In addition, when the torque-generator output torque is proportional to the command-signal input within a negligibly small uncertainty, the controlled-member angular velocity may be regarded as proportional to the command signal. If the base does not rotate inertially, an indication of the angular displacement of the controlled member with respect to the base represents the integral of command-signal input variations with respect to time. Conversely, an integral of the command signal with respect to time is a direct measure of the angular displacement of the controlled member with respect to inertial space about the gyro input axis. For this reason, an arrangement of the kind illustrated by Fig. 7-4 is called a single-axis *space integrator*. The three gyro units of a three-axis inertial reference package that changes its orientation with respect to inertial space under command-signal inputs may be regarded as a three-axis space integrator, in analogy with the single-axis case. However, while a simple linear differential equation describes the single-axis case, a linear differential matrix equation is required for a one-equation description of the three-axis case, to take interaxial coupling into account.

Specific-force receivers[9, 24]

The measurement of force on a moving vehicle for navigation purposes may be done with accelerometers. This term admits of several possible definitions, but usually implies the measurement of the force in terms of the displacement of an elastically-restrained seismic mass. It is desirable to be less specific in discussing force measurement, for many classes of instruments fall outside the spring-restrained-mass category. It should be noted also that the *specific force*, the force per unit mass, is to be measured. Thus, the words *specific-force receiver* are used here to describe this broad class of instruments.

Specific-force receivers all depend upon the resultant body force per unit mass due to the combined effects of gravitational fields and the inertia-reaction to linear acceleration. In order to realize practical instruments for indicating or measuring specific force along any established direction, it is necessary to balance the resultant effect of specific force on a mass that acts as a seismic element. (The name *seismic element* implies that the mass plays the role of the suspended mass used in conventional seismographs.)

Many arrangements are available for balancing the effects of specific force acting on the seismic element of a specific-force receiver. Linear or torsional springs are commonly used to provide an elastic-balance seismic-element force. The specific force is indicated as a spring deflection from a reference position. The change in the natural frequency of a stretched elastic filament, under a load determined by the specific force acting on a seismic element, may also be used. Or, a seismic element may be restrained to a reference position by a force- or torque-generator, which is energized with electrical-current commands originating as signals representing the seismic-element displacement. The output here is the electrical signal required to null the seismic-element displacement.

Elastic materials exhibit hysteresis with varying stress, and creep under long-continued stress. Torque and force generators are difficult to design for constant sensitivity over a wide range of outputs and, in any case, require calibration at many points if high accuracy is to be achieved.

Gyroscopic torque from a rotor spinning at constant speed also may be used to restrain a seismic mass. The torque output from a rotor-and-gimbal structure designed, for high rigidity, as a precise single-degree-of-freedom gyro with small output-axis uncertainty torque, is accurately proportional to the angular velocity about the input axis over very wide ranges of operation. The single quantity controlling the sensitivity of a given gyroscopic-element restraint is the frequency of the electrical driving power for the spinning rotor. Hysteresis and saturation effects cannot occur, as they must for end-range inputs to the elastically restrained units already mentioned. This means that the input-axis angular *velocity* of the gyroscopic unit is accurately proportional to the restraint *torque* imposed on a seismic element and therefore the *angle* that the element turns through with respect to inertial space is exactly proportional to the *integral* of the specific-force input.

Figure 7-5 is a pictorial-schematic representation of a specific-force integrating receiver with a gyroscopic element restraining the seismic element. The seismic element is shown as being provided by the addition of a symmetrical mass to the rotor. This mass is located so that the center of gravity of the rotor is shifted away from the output axis along the spin axis. In another configuration that is used, this mass is placed directly on the gimbal that supports the rotor.

Except for the addition of the seismic element, the specific-force integrating receiver of Fig. 7-5 is similar to the single-axis inertial-space angle integrator of Fig. 7-4. Starting with the seismic-element arm aligned with the spin reference axis of the gyro unit, a specific-force component along the input axis of the gyro unit causes a force to act at the center of gravity of the float as well as at the center of buoyancy. The resulting torque on the float causes the spin axis to move away from the spin reference axis and the signal-generator output to change

Table 7-1. Earth angular velocity units.

Unit Name	Unit Symbol	Degrees/Hour	Minutes of Arc/Hour	Seconds of Arc/Hour	Radians/Hour	Radians/Second	Milliradians/Second
Earth Rate Unit	eru	15	900	54,000	0.26	0.73×10^{-4}	0.73×10^{-1}
Deci Earth Rate Unit	deru	1.5	90	5,400	0.26×10^{-1}	0.73×10^{-5}	0.73×10^{-2}
Centi Earth Rate Unit	ceru	0.15	9	540	0.26×10^{-2}	0.73×10^{-6}	0.73×10^{-3}
Milli Earth Rate Unit	meru	0 015	0.9	54	0.26×10^{-3}	$0 73 \times 10^{-7}$	0.73×10^{-4}
Deci Milli Earth Rate Unit	d meru	0 0015	0.09	5 4	$0 26 \times 10^{-4}$	0.73×10^{-8}	$0 73 \times 10^{-5}$
Centi Milli Earth Rate Unit	c meru	0 00015	0 009	0 54	$0 26 \times 10^{-5}$	$0 73 \times 10^{-9}$	0.73×10^{-6}
Milli Milli Earth Rate Unit	m meru	0 000015	0.0009	0 054	0.26×10^{-6}	$0 73 \times 10^{-10}$	$0 73 \times 10^{-7}$

from its null level. This signal acts through the servodrive system to rotate the controlled member with an angular velocity that produces the gyro output torque required to balance the torque due to specific force acting on the seismic element. This angular velocity is with respect to inertial space, which is effectively the same as angular velocity with respect to the base when the base is fixed to a nonrotating inertial reference package. (One of the important advantages of systems with stabilized inertial packages, as compared with systems in which vehicle-structure-mounted instruments are employed, is that specific-force integrators based on pendulous gyro units may be applied without correcting specific-force indications for vehicle-motion effects.)

Quantitative performance measures and design specifications

It is instructive to review the numerical values involved and the region of mechanical uncertainty that must be realized, in a general way, to meet the specifications for high-quality inertial systems. A great number of difficult problems have to be solved before satisfactory equipment is operational, but the principal limiting factor in any inertial system, given the best possible design and execution in all other aspects, is the uncertainty in center-of-mass position of rotor-carrying gimbal structures. This is because these uncertainties in gyros result in drift-rate uncertainties, while these uncertainties in specific-force receivers

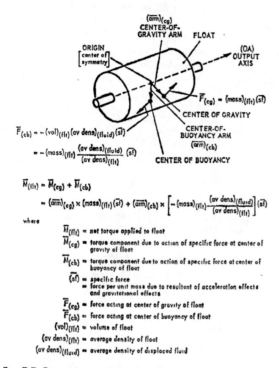

$$\bar{M}_{(flt)} = \bar{M}_{(cg)} + \bar{M}_{(cb)}$$

$$= (\overline{arm})_{(cg)} \times (mass)_{(flt)} (\bar{sf}) + (\overline{arm})_{(cb)} \times \left[-(mass)_{(flt)} \frac{(av\ dens)_{(fluid)}}{(av\ dens)_{(flt)}} \right] (\bar{sf})$$

where

$\bar{M}_{(flt)}$ = net torque applied to float

$\bar{M}_{(cg)}$ = torque component due to action of specific force at center of gravity of float

$\bar{M}_{(cb)}$ = torque component due to action of specific force at center of buoyancy of float

$(\bar{sf})$ = specific force
= force per unit mass due to resultant of acceleration effects and gravitational effects

$\bar{F}_{(cg)}$ = force acting at center of gravity of float

$\bar{F}_{(cb)}$ = force acting at center of buoyancy of float

$(vol)_{(flt)}$ = volume of float

$(av\ dens)_{(flt)}$ = average density of float

$(av\ dens)_{(fluid)}$ = average density of displaced fluid

Fig. 7-7. Factors controlling the torque about the geometrical symmetry of the float that are due to positions of the center of mass and the center of buoyancy.

render calibration uncertain. Both uncertainties give rise to ineradicable errors in position and heading indication. To give the reader a feeling for the magnitudes that must be considered, Table 7-1 gives names, symbols, and magnitudes in various units of the angular velocity associated with the earth's daily rotation. Figure 7-7 gives vector expressions for the torques acting on a gyro-unit float due to displacements of the center of mass and the center of buoyancy from the geometrical center of symmetry of the float. Figure 7-8 applies the results of Fig. 7-7 to a typical gyro unit whose float has a weight of five hundred grams and whose rotor has an angular velocity of 10^6 gram centimeters-squared per second. When this unit is subjected to the maximum effect of the earth's gravity acting on a mass unbalance of the float, the drift angular velocity in radians per second is equal to one-half the length of the arm

Assumed conditions:

Specific force

specific force = $(\overline{sf}) = \overline{g}$; g = 980 centimeters/(second)^2

Float characteristics

mass of float = $(mass)_{(flt)}$ = 500 grams
center-of-buoyancy arm = $(arm)_{(cb)}$ = 0; hence $M_{(cb)}$ (see Fig. 24) is zero
center-of-gravity arm, $(arm)_{(cg)}$, is to be determined; $(\overline{arm})_{(cg)} \perp (OA)$
$(arm)_{(cg)}$ and (OA) both horizontal

Gyro-element characteristics

angular momentum = H = 10^6 gram (centimeters)^2/second

Derivation of drift rate — center-of-gravity arm relationship:

From Fig. 19, the torque applied to the float about the gyro output axis due to an input angular velocity, $\overline{W}_{(gu)(IA)}$, applied to the gyro unit about its input axis is

$$\overline{M}_{(ge)(out)} = \overline{H} \times \overline{W}_{(gu)(IA)}$$

or

$$M_{(ge)(out)} = H W_{(gu)(IA)}$$

since $\overline{H}$ is very nearly perpendicular to the input axis in a single-degree-of-freedom gyro unit. This means that the drift rate, $W_{(drift)(gu)}$, corresponding to an undesired torque, $\overline{M}_{(cg)}$, about the gyro output axis resulting from the action of specific force on the float mass when the center-of-gravity arm is not zero (see Fig. 24) is given by the relationship

$$W_{(drift)(gu)} = \frac{M_{(cg)}}{H} \tag{1}$$

Under the conditions noted above, Fig. 24 shows that $M_{(cg)}$ can be expressed as

$$M_{(cg)} = (arm)_{(cg)}(mass)_{(flt)}(sf) \tag{2}$$

Substitution of Eq. (2) into Eq. (1) gives

$$W_{(drift)(gu)} = \frac{(arm)_{(cg)}(mass)_{(flt)}(sf)}{H}$$

For the representative unit being considered here,

$$W_{(drift)(gu)} = \frac{(500 \; grams)(980 \; centimeters/(second)^2)}{10^6 \; gram \; (centimeters)^2/second} (arm)_{(cg)}$$

which reduces to

$$\boxed{W_{(drift)(gu)} \cong \frac{1}{2} (arm)_{(cg)}}$$

where $W_{(drift)(gu)}$ is in radians per second if $(arm)_{(cg)}$ is in centimeters.

Fig. 7-8. Typical relationship between drift rate and center-of-gravity position for a representative single-degree-of-freedom gyro unit under one earth gravity.

between the center of symmetry and the center of gravity in centimeters. Table 7-2 summarizes the magnitudes of the center-of-gravity arm that correspond to various drift rates for the example treated in Fig. 7-7. For example, this arm in the case of a marginal inertial-quality gyro unit (drift rate equal to one meru) is about one-half of one-tenth of a microinch, which is about fifteen ångstrom units (one ångström unit equals 10^{-8} centimeter) and about five times the distance between the atoms in the crystal lattices of steel, aluminum, and beryllium, which are the materials commonly used for the structures of high-performance inertial instruments.

If the lengths of the center-of-gravity arms are considered as not fixed but uncertain, so that they contribute uncertainty to the gyro drift rate, then the data of Table 7-2 can also be considered to be that of drift-rate

Table 7-2. Center-of-mass positions with respect to the output axis that correspond to various drift rates; based on the relationship developed in Fig. 25 for a representative gyro unit.

Drift Rate		Center-of-Mass Position with Respect to Output Axis $(arm)_{(cg)}$			
in Earth Angular Velocity Units	in $\frac{Radians}{Second}$	in Centimeters	in Microinches	in Angstroms	in Lattice Constants (approx) of Aluminum, Steel, or Beryllium*
1 eru	0.73×10^{-4}	1.46×10^{-4}	57.5	1.46×10^4	$\approx 0.5 \times 10^4$ or 5000
1 deru	0.73×10^{-5}	1.46×10^{-5}	5.75	1.46×10^3	0.5×10^3 500
1 ceru	0.73×10^{-6}	1.46×10^{-6}	0.575	1.46×10^2	0.5×10^2 50
1 meru	0.73×10^{-7}	1.46×10^{-7}	0.0575	1.46×10	0.5×10 5
1 d meru	0.73×10^{-8}	1.46×10^{-8}	0.00575	1.46	0.5 1/2
1 c meru	0.73×10^{-9}	1.46×10^{-9}	0.000575	0.146	0.05 1/20
1 m meru	0.73×10^{-10}	1.46×10^{-10}	0.0000575	0.0146	0.005 1/200

* The lattice constants of aluminum, steel and beryllium are approximately 3 angstrom units, that is, 3×10^{-8} centimeter

uncertainty versus center-of-gravity arm-length uncertainty. The numbers in the lowest line of Table 7-2 are for the case when the gyro unit of Fig. 7-7 has a drift-rate uncertainty of one millimeru, which would generally be satisfactory for inertial purposes. The small arm uncertainties that are allowable in this typical unit used for illustration purposes emphasize the difficulties of gyro-unit design. It is to be noted that *arm uncertainties of the same order of magnitude apply to all gyroscopic instruments,* so that changing construction details, the number of degrees of freedom, or the method of suspension cannot solve the basic problem of gyro drift. Only careful design, good materials, and excellent techniques in manufacture and use can meet the needs of inertial guidance.

Essential features of single-degree-of-freedom floated integrating gyro units[24]

Gyro units intended for inertial-reference applications may be designed in many ways. The example to be reviewed here is the single-degree-of-freedom floated integrating gyro unit with the features illustrated by the diagram of Fig. 7-9. The gyro rotor with its multiphase, alternating-current, synchronous drive motor is mounted in a gimbal that is integral with and internal to the float. Symmetrical projections from either end of the cylindrical float carry pivot shafts that fit into watch-jewel-type gimbal bearings of highly-polished tungsten carbide. Spring-loaded balls of tungsten carbide act in conjunction with the spherical ends of the pivots to provide end support. The floated assembly is enclosed in a cylindrical case with a clearance of about 0.005 inch between the float and the case. An electrical-heater spirally wound on

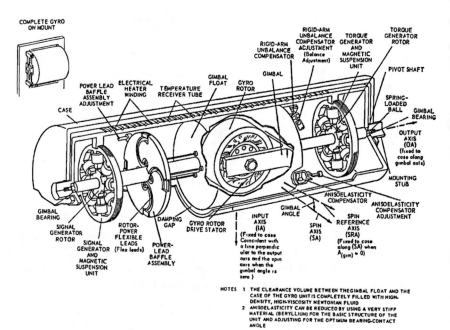

Fig. 7-9a The MIT single-degree-of-freedom floated integrating gyro unit.

the outside of the case controls the temperature of the entire gyro unit. In operation, a microswitch in the heater-winding circuit is actuated by a bellows (not shown in Fig. 7-9) whose action is governed by the expansion and contraction of fluid contained in a copper-tube temperature receiver, also spirally wound on the case. The clearance volume between the float and the case is filled with a particle-free, gas-free, high-density, high-viscosity fluid with Newtonian behavior, so that the shear drag is accurately equal to the shear gradient. By design and adjustments carried out during assembly, the average density of the float is made substantially equal to the average density of the fluid. A final, highly-accurate adjustment of average float density may be made by varying the temperature setting of the thermoswitch. In practice, thermal control is more satisfactory if a single heat-exchange system is built into the package upon which the gyro units and specific-force receivers are mounted. Then, by the forced circulation of a liquid or gaseous heat-transfer medium, very accurate control of temperature is possible for all components simultaneously with a single thermal-switch element.

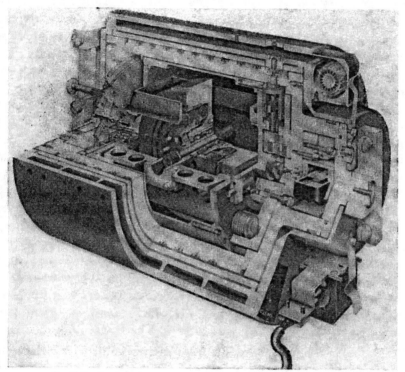

Fig. 7-9b. Sectioned view of MIT single-axis integrating gyro unit.

The float carries rigid-arm unbalance compensators in the form of screws that may be adjusted from outside the case under operating conditions. Anisoelasticity compensators with provision for external adjustments are also sometimes attached to the float. Each anisoelasticity compensator consists of small weights fixed to the float by means of cantilever springs attached to a rotatable mount that may be adjusted so that the shift in float mass due to spring deflections that result from a given specific force just compensates for the effects of elastic deformations in the float under the same specific force. Changes in the center-of-gravity arm away from alignment with the direction of the applied specific force occur when the elastic coefficients of the float structure along the input axis and the spin reference axis are different. Arm distortions of this kind have the effect of carrying the center of mass to one side of the specific-force direction, so that the float is subjected to a torque that depends on elastic deformations of the parts that support the rotor inside the float shell. This anisoelasticity torque has a magnitude that varies with the *square* of the magnitude of the specific force acting, because the effective arm is proportional to the magnitude of the applied force, and the force that acts at the end of the arm to produce the torque is also proportional to the magnitude of the applied force. When properly adjusted, the anisoelasticity compensators operate by generating a specific-force torque from the elastically supported masses that is equal in magnitude and opposite in direction to the anisoelastic torque on the float itself. For certain applications, it is possible to use materials and select design proportions for the gyro structure that reduce anisoelasticity torques to levels that are satisfactory without the use of anisoelasticity compensators.

Flexible leads for rotor power having their outer ends attached to electrical terminals that are fixed to the outer circumference of the power-lead baffle assembly are shown in Fig. 7-9. Four leads are used to ground the float structure and to supply power for a three-phase drive-motor stator. The leads are formed of wire whose density is very close to the density of the fluid under operating conditions. With a fluorolube fluid having a density of approximately 2 grams per cubic centimeter, either aluminum (density 2.8 g/cm^3) or beryllium (density 1.8 g/cm^3) are suitable materials for flexible power leads. The leads are formed into semicircles, which, unstressed, exactly match with the terminals on the float and on the baffle. The angular distortions to which the leads are subjected by gyro operation are less than one minute of arc. The maximum possible torque exerted on the float is very small. This small torque is achieved in practice by means of an externally operated power-lead baffle assembly adjustment that makes it possible to rotate the baffle with respect to the case with the unit in normal operation. The four leads are located in grooves on the face of the baffle that are wide and deep enough to prevent physical contact with the leads from occurring. These grooves insure that the leads are never damaged by shrinkage cracks in large blocks of solidified fluid during storage of the units at low temperatures.

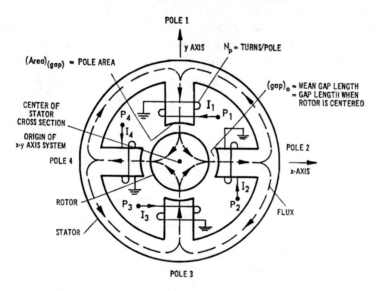

CROSS SECTION OF MAGNETIC SUSPENSION UNIT

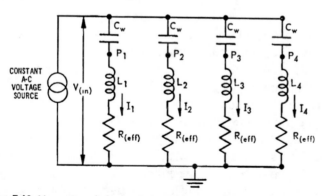

ELECTRICAL CIRCUIT OF MAGNETIC SUSPENSION UNIT

Fig. 7-10. Magnetic and electrical circuit diagrams for magnetic suspension units.

Magnetic suspension of the float[25, 26, 27]

If the excitation, or primary winding, of each microsyn is suitably connected to a common excitation source through a pair of respective passive capacitor networks each rotor is supported radially, in the plane

H

perpendicular to the output axis of the unit, by a quasi-elastic force. This magnetic support assists the viscous damping force acting on the float to maintain orthogonality among the output axis, input axis and the spin reference axis. This minimizes not only gyro coupling uncertainties, but also uncertainty signals and torques caused by the radial displacement of the respective microsyn rotors. This magnetic support also prevents any gimbal-bearing contact at the pivot-and-jewel support, even when the float is subjected to large accelerations up to some maximum specified value.

The quasi-elastic radial support is realized because the quiescent air-gap magnetic energy is made to readjust itself, so as to provide a magnetic force on the rotor (proportional to its radial displacement with respect to the stator) in the direction opposite to the applied force. This is done by setting the values of the capacitors C_w in Fig. 7-10 near the 'half-power point', where the quiescent voltage across each primary coil is always greater than the corresponding voltage across the condenser.

The microsyns consist of 8-pole stator cores wherein each primary winding serves as the excitation winding for the signal generator and torque generator respectively, and concurrently as the magnetic support winding for each end of the floated gimbal. Thus the primary flux density performs the double function of being the energy source for the magnetic support as well as for the signal generator and torque generator output signal voltage and output torque respectively.

The microsyns usually have identical cores, windings, air gaps, etc.; mounting them 'back-to-back' with respect to the floated gimbal assures that residual or reaction torques due to environmental changes or stray fields tend to compensate each other to some extent.

Figure 7-10 gives magnetic and electrical circuit diagrams for the magnetic suspension units of Fig. 7-9. Four poles are shown in the stator for purposes of illustration, although in practice any convenient number may be used. The stator and rotor are formed of high-permeability, low-hysteresis material that may be either laminated or sintered. Each salient pole carries a winding, and all windings are connected to an alternating-current, constant-frequency voltage source. Capacitors are used in series with the windings to give current variations with gap length of the type illustrated by the curve of Fig. 7-11. The tuning used is such that a small decrease in gap length under any given pole causes a relatively large decrease in the current through the coil of the associated pole. This decrease in current causes the flux through the gap to decrease. There is a corresponding reduction in attractive force on the rotor, since this force varies as the square of the current. The increase in gap length, on the side of the rotor opposite which the gap decrease occurs, causes the force on the rotor to become greater by a process similar to that described for the decreased gap. The resultant effect of

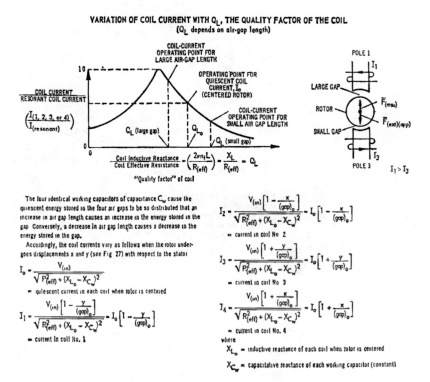

The four identical working capacitors of capacitance C_w cause the quiescent energy stored in the four air gaps to be so distributed that an increase in air gap length causes an increase in the energy stored in the gap. Conversely, a decrease in air gap length causes a decrease in the energy stored in the gap.

Accordingly, the coil currents vary as follows when the rotor undergoes displacements x and y (see Fig 27) with respect to the stator

$$I_0 = \frac{V_{(in)}}{\sqrt{R_{(eff)}^2 + (X_{L_0} - X_{C_w})^2}}$$

= quiescent current in each coil when rotor is centered

$$I_1 = \frac{V_{(in)}\left[1 - \frac{y}{(gap)_0}\right]}{\sqrt{R_{(eff)}^2 + (X_{L_0} - X_{C_w})^2}} = I_0\left[1 - \frac{y}{(gap)_0}\right]$$

= current in coil No. 1

$$I_2 = \frac{V_{(in)}\left[1 - \frac{x}{(gap)_0}\right]}{\sqrt{R_{(eff)}^2 + (X_{L_0} - X_{C_w})^2}} = I_0\left[1 - \frac{x}{(gap)_0}\right]$$

= current in coil No 2

$$I_3 = \frac{V_{(in)}\left[1 + \frac{y}{(gap)_0}\right]}{\sqrt{R_{(eff)}^2 + (X_{L_0} - X_{C_w})^2}} = I_0\left[1 + \frac{y}{(gap)_0}\right]$$

= current in coil No 3

$$I_4 = \frac{V_{(in)}\left[1 + \frac{x}{(gap)_0}\right]}{\sqrt{R_{(eff)}^2 + (X_{L_0} - X_{C_w})^2}} = I_0\left[1 + \frac{x}{(gap)_0}\right]$$

= current in coil No. 4

where

X_{L_0} = inductive reactance of each coil when rotor is centered

X_{C_w} = capacitative reactance of each working capacitor (constant)

Fig. 7-11. Current-variation curve and equations for magnetic suspension.

the electrical and magnetic actions that occur in magnetic suspension units is a system of elastic (but very 'stiff') forces that acts to maintain the rotor in a symmetrical position with respect to the stator pole faces. Figure 7-12 gives the performance equation of the magnetic suspension unit in terms of rotor-displacement input and force output.

One of the great advantages of electromagnetic suspension units with the features of Figs. 7-10 through 7-12 is that the circuits associated with opposite poles may be used in bridge configurations to form *electromagnetic micrometers* that can supply information on rotor positions with uncertainty levels in the region of one microinch. The known pivot-and-jewel clearances may be used to calibrate the micrometer arrangements. Thus, the suspension circuits themselves may be used as measuring elements in selecting the tuning capacitors to place rotors accurately in their positions of symmetry with respect to the stators.

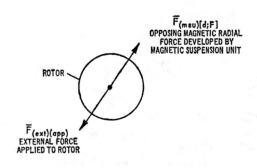

$$\bar{F}_{(msu)[d;F]} = \bar{F}_{(ext)(app)} = S_{(msu)[d;F]}\bar{d}$$

where

$S_{(msu)[d,F]}$ = displacement input – force output sensitivity of magnetic suspension unit

$\bar{d} = ix + jy$ = net displacement of rotor resulting from applied external force and opposing magnetic radial force

i and j = vectors of unit length along x and y axes, respectively

As a result of the energy changes that take place in the air gaps with a change in gap length, the sensitivity is effectively constant and is given by the relationship

$$S_{(msu)[d,F]} = \left[\frac{N_p I_o}{(gap)_o}\right]^2 \frac{(Area)_{(gap)}}{(gap)_o}(Q_{L_o} - 2)$$

where

$$Q_{L_o} = \frac{2\pi n_f L_o}{R_{(eff)}}$$

n_f = frequency of the constant a-c voltage input $V_{(in)}$
L_o = inductance of each coil when rotor is centered
$R_{(eff)}$ = effective resistance of each coil (constant)

I_o = quiescent (centered-rotor) coil current

and the other quantities are as defined in the diagrams of the magnetic suspension unit that appear in Figs. 27 and 28.

Fig. 7-12. Displacement-force performance equation for the magnetic suspension unit.

In operation, magnetic suspension units provide no more than a few grams force for each ten-thousandth-of-an-inch change in position of the rotor with respect to the stator. This force may be greatly increased by the use of servo-type feedback circuits between arrangements providing electromagnetic micrometer-type signals and the coils, but considerable complications are introduced, and the advantage to be gained is small. In any case, the hydrodynamic drag force produced by fluid flow in the clearance volume when the float changes its position within the case is very large compared with magnetic-suspension forces. This means that the suspension must act by slowly bringing the float to its position of symmetry with respect to the case and maintaining this position over long time periods against the small forces from residual buoyancy imperfections and mass unbalances. When the float is free from all contact with the case in its position of symmetry, the forces and torques on the float are due to pressure gradients and viscous shear, with uncertainty effects from rubbing friction reduced to levels that are negligibly small for practical purposes. At the same time, the float supporting forces from the pressure gradients that give buoyancy, and the viscous flow that forces movement to be very slow, give the float great ability to operate without being affected by violent shocks, high accelerations, or severe vibration.

The testing of gyro units[28]

It is instructive to consider the methods of laboratory test of, as an example, single-degree-of-freedom gyros. Testing, in effect, dissects the complex operational situation into cause-and-effect sequences. It will be clear from the preceding discussion of residual-mass-unbalance and anisoelasticity correction that the test process has clear limits, and that, below certain levels, the describing parameters of a gyro exhibit a random behavior.

In the gyro test laboratory, single-axis base-motion-isolation and command-signal systems are used to test, calibrate and study integrating gyroscopes. The single-axis system consists of (a) a turntable, whose axis of rotation may be fixed in a given orientation with respect to the local vertical and the earth's polar axis, and (b) a set of electrical and electronic equipment to provide the required excitations for gyro operation and for single-axis stabilization. This equipment, which will not be detailed here, provides gyro-heater power, gyro-wheel power, signal-generator excitation and torque-generator excitation. Stabilization is accomplished by means of a closed-loop servo system from the gyro through a servo amplifier to a turntable drive motor. An angular rate about the input axis of the gyro, which is mounted on the turntable with its input axis parallel to the axis of rotation of the turntable, or any modifying inputs that produce a torque about the output axis, result in a signal-generator output signal. This signal is amplified and applied to the turntable drive motor to rotate the turntable in such a direction as to return the gyro float to its null position and thus cancel the inputs.

A *perfect* gyro mounted on the turntable with its input axis parallel to the axis of rotation of the turntable and parallel to the earth's polar axis (see Figs. 7-13 and 7-14) could cause the turntable to remain fixed with respect to inertial space, i.e., the turntable rotates with respect to the earth at the earth's sidereal rate. With an *actual* gyro unit, the turntable does not rotate at sidereal rate, because of unbalance torques about the output axis of the gyro that add to the torque exerted by the earth.

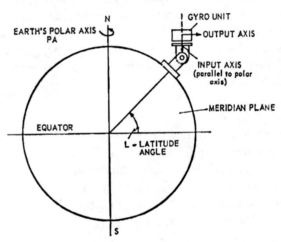

Fig. 7-13. Orientation of the gyro unit with respect to the earth for a servo run with IA∥PA—South.

The turntable rate is measured with respect to the earth; earth rate is subtracted, and the torque about the output axis of the gyro due to the unbalance torques may be calculated, as a function of gravity and the angle of the turntable rotation with respect to a given reference orientation. The turntable angle can be measured, while it rotates, by a photoelectric device triggered by a beam of light passed by a graduated glass dial mounted concentric with the turntable rotational axis. The output of the photoelectric scale reader is amplified and trips an elapsed-time recorder. Thus, the average rate of the turntable for any given angular rotation of the turntable may be calculated by subtracting the times at which the prints occurred on the elapsed time recorder.

Before proceeding to the computation of turntable rate in meru and the development of the unbalance equations, it is necessary that several quantities be defined.

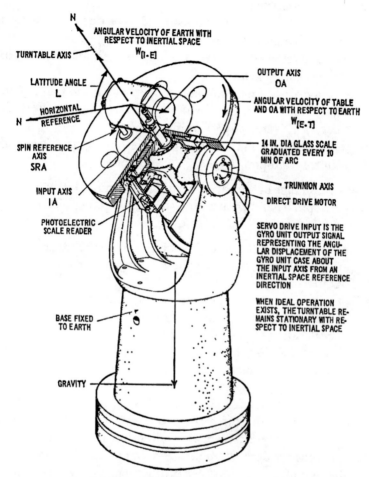

Fig. 7-14. Pictorial diagram of the servo turntable

A. TURNTABLE ANGLE

L = geographic latitude angle

ø = turntable angle in degrees measured from a zero reference (west).

B. GYRO AXES (see Fig. 7-14).

The output axis OA, spin reference axis SRA, and input axis IA have been defined. They, in turn, define the positive direction of rotation of the gyro wheel. This direction of rotation will be assumed in what follows, unless otherwise stated.

C. SOURCES OF UNBALANCE

The unbalance of the gyro float is assumed to be due to the following sources (listed with a consistent set of suitable units):

M_R = torque composed of power-lead torque and microsyn reaction torque. Units: dyne-cm.

$(U)m_{SRA}$ = moment of mass unbalance fixed along the spin reference axis. Units: gram-cm. [Note that $(U)m_{SRA}f_{SRA} = (U)M_{SRA}$, where f_{SRA} is the *specific force* along SRA.]

$(U)m_{IA}$ = moment of mass unbalance fixed along the input axis. Units: gram-cm.

$\dfrac{1}{k_{SRA}}$ = compliance of the wheel, bearing, and gimbal structure along the spin reference axis due to a force acting along the spin reference axis. Units: cm/dyne.

$\dfrac{1}{k_{IA}}$ = compliance of the wheel, bearing, and gimbal structure along the input axis due to a force acting along the input axis. Units: cm/dyne.

m = mass of the wheel, bearing, and gimbal structure displaced from the output axis in the IA-SRA plane. Units: gram.

g = acceleration of gravity. Units: cm/sec.^{2}

It will be assumed that the sum of the unbalance torques about the output axis is always less than the gyro precessional torque due to earth rate.

The purpose of Derivation Summary 7-4 is to derive a set of unbalance equations for the servo turntable test. The algebraic sign of each component in the unbalance equation has physical significance, and the equations are derived on the basis that positive mass unbalance exists. If the sign of the results of the computing agrees with the derived sign, i.e., minus $(U)m_{SRA}$ from the computing agrees with the minus $(U)m_{SRA}$ occurring in the derivation, then a mass unbalance $(U)m_{SRA}$ exists along the *positive* direction of SRA.

It is intended that this physical significance be maintained even if the gyro wheel direction is reversed or the orientation of the unit is changed with respect to the turntable. There are two reasons for using this approach. First, it may be necessary at any time to make mechanical corrections for $(U)m_{SRA}$ and $(U)m_{IA}$ by turning the balance

Input Axis IA Vertical

IA is aligned parallel to the axis of rotation of the turntable and directed into the turntable. At the start of e run, the output axis, OA, is pointing west in alignment with the zero reference orientation of the turn-ble.

1. IA vertical down, wheel positive:

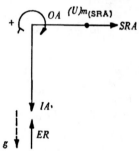

Fig. 7-15. IA vertical down, wheel positive.

Earth-rate input is negative and creates a negative torque about OA. The mass unbalance $(U)m_{(SRA)}$ eates a positive torque $g(U)m_{(SRA)}$ about OA. The total torque about OA is less than the torque due to rth rate and the turntable rate is, therefore, less than earth rate. The power-lead torque is independent gyro unit orientation and is considered a positive torque for purposes of analysis. Both $(U)M_R$ and $^{U)}m_{(SRA)}$ are independent of the turntable angle ϕ, and a plot of unbalance versus turntable angle should a straight line. The unbalance torque uncertainty is

$$(U)M = +(U)M_R + g(U)m_{(SRA)}$$

2. IA vertical down, wheel negative:

Earth-rate input is negative and creates positive torque about OA. $(U)M_R$ and $g(U)m_{(SRA)}$ have not anged and so add to the effect of the earth-rate input. The turntable must rotate faster than earth rate a clockwise direction as before.

$$(U)M = -[+(U)M_R + g(U)m_{(SRA)}] = -(U)M_R - g(U)m_{(SRA)}$$

The negative signs indicate that both $(U)M_R$ and $g(U)m_{(SRA)}$ are positive torques for the standard con-ion.

3. IA vertical up, wheel positive:

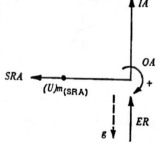

Fig. 7-16. IA vertical up, wheel positive.

Derivation Summary 7-4. The unbalance equations. (Page 1 of 3)

Earth-rate input is positive and creates a positive torque about OA. $(U)M_R$ is positive about OA, and $g(U)m_{(SRA)}$ is negative about OA. If $g(U)m_{(SRA)}$ is greater than $(U)M_R$, the turntable must rotate at a rate less than earth rate, and conversely. The net torque uncertainty is

$$(U)M = -(U)M_R + g(U)m_{(SRA)}$$

The same technique will be used throughout the procedure to determine the signs.

4. IA vertical up, wheel negative:

$$(U)M = +(U)M_R - g(U)m_{(SRA)}$$

B. IA Horizontal — South

IA is aligned parallel to the axis of rotation of the turntable and directed into the turntable. At the start of the run, OA is pointing west in alignment with the zero reference on the turntable.

1. IA Horizontal — South, wheel rotation positive:

$$(U)M = +(U)M_R - g(U)m_{(IA)} \cos \phi$$

2. IA Horizontal — South, wheel rotation negative:

$$(U)M = -(U)M_R + g(U)m_{(IA)} \cos \phi_.$$

3. IA Horizontal — North, wheel rotation positive:

$$(U)M = -(U)M_R - g(U)m_{(IA)} \cos \phi$$

4. IA Horizontal — North, wheel rotation negative:

$$(U)M = +(U)M_R + g(U)m_{(IA)} \cos \phi$$

C. IA∥PA — South

IA is aligned parallel to the axis of rotation of the turntable and directed into the turntable. At the start of the run, OA is pointing west in alignment with the zero reference on the turntable.

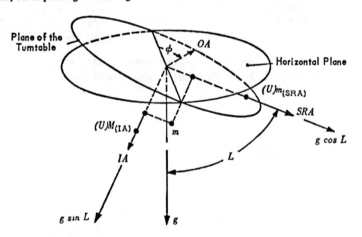

Fig. 7-17. IA∥EA — South, wheel positive.
Derivation Summary 7-4. The unbalance equations. (Page 2 of 3)

1. IA||PA – South, wheel rotation positive: Earth-rate input is negative and produces a negative torque about the output axis. Then, $g(U)m_{(SRA)} \sin \beta$ produces a positive torque about the output axis so that it subtracts from the effect of earth rate and causes the turntable to turn more slowly than earth rate. This results in a positive calculated rate, $+g(U)m_{(SRA)} \sin L$. However, the torque produced due to $(U)m_{(IA)}$ is function of turntable angle ϕ and results in an unbalanced torque equal to $-g(U)m_{IA} \cos L \cos \phi$.

$$\frac{1}{k_{(SRA)}} \, m g \cos L \cos \phi \; = \; \text{displacement along SRA due to } g \cos L \cos \phi$$

$$+ \frac{1}{k_{(SRA)}} \, m^2 g^2 \sin L \cos L \cos \phi \; = \; \text{positive torque about OA}$$

$$\frac{1}{k_{(IA)}} \, mg \sin L \; = \; \text{displacement along IA due to } g \sin L$$

$$- \frac{1}{k_{(IA)}} \, m^2 g^2 \sin L \cos L \cos \phi \; = \; \text{negative torque about OA}$$

The sum of the uncertainty torques is

$$(U)M \; = \; +(U)M_R + g(U)m_{(SRA)} \sin L + \left\{ \left[\frac{\frac{1}{k_{(SRA)}} - \frac{1}{k_{(IA)}}}{2} \right] m^2 g^2 \sin 2L \; - \; g(U)m_{(IA)} \cos L \right\} \cos \phi$$

2. IA||PA – South, wheel rotation negative:

$$(U)M \; = \; -(U)M_R - g(U)m_{(SRA)} \sin L - \left\{ \left[\frac{\frac{1}{k_{(SRA)}} - \frac{1}{k_{(IA)}}}{2} \right] m^2 g^2 \sin 2L \; - \; g(U)m_{(IA)} \cos L \right\} \cos \phi$$

3. IA||PA – North, wheel rotation positive:

$$(U)M \; = \; -(U)M_R + g(U)m_{(SRA)} \sin L - \left\{ \left[\frac{\frac{1}{k_{(SRA)}} - \frac{1}{k_{(IA)}}}{2} \right] m^2 g^2 \sin 2L \; + \; g(U)m_{(IA)} \cos L \right\} \cos \phi$$

4. IA||PA – North, wheel rotation negative:

$$(U)M \; = \; +(U)M_R - g(U)m_{(SRA)} \sin L + \left\{ \left[\frac{\frac{1}{k_{(SRA)}} - \frac{1}{k_{(IA)}}}{2} \right] m^2 g^2 \sin 2L \; + \; g(U)m_{(IA)} \cos L \right\} \cos \phi$$

Derivation Summary 7-4. The unbalance equations. (Page 3 of 3)

adjustments on the float, in which case, the mass to be corrected for is properly located physically in the gyro. Second, it greatly simplifies the computations, since it is sufficient to set up a single computing procedure whose results are interpreted by applying the appropriate unbalance equation.

Figure 7-14 shows the standard mounting orientation of the gyro with respect to the turntable. The input axis is aligned parallel to the axis of rotation of the turntable and directed into the turntable, and the output axis is aligned with the zero-degree reading on the turntable. At the beginning of each servo run, the turntable is set so that the output axis of the gyro is horizontal and pointing west. When the gyro is so mounted, the earth-rate input is negative. The turntable rotates (during the servo run) opposite to earth's rate and creates a positive rate input to the gyro. If one looks down upon the earth from the North Star, the earth turns counterclockwise while the turntable turns clockwise; this is defined as a positive turntable rotation. The rate input to the gyro with respect to inertial space is then the turntable rate minus earth rate.

During the performance tests on a gyro unit, it may be desirable to apply compensating torques by means of the torque generator. In Table 7-3, compensating torques listed are for positive unbalances as

Table 7-3. Signs of compensating torques.

IA vertical up, wheel positive
    Positive torque
IA vertical up, wheel negative·
    Negative torque
IA horizontal — South, wheel positive:
    Negative torque
IA horizontal — South, wheel negative:
    Positive torque
IA horizontal — North, wheel positive·
    Positive torque
IA horizontal — North, wheel negative·
    Negative torque
IA||PA — South, wheel positive·
    Negative torque
IA||PA — South, wheel negative·
    Positive torque
IA||PA — North, wheel positive:
    Positive torque
IA||PA — North, wheel negative:
    Negative torque

read from the plots of drift versus turntable orientation. When IA is along the vertical and positive down with the wheel rotation positive, the unbalance torque $(U)M_R+g(U)m_{SRA}$ is positive; a negative torque should be applied for correction. When IA is along the vertical and positive down, with the wheel negative, the unbalance torque $(U)M_R-g(U)m_{SRA}$ is positive, but the correction torques to be listed are for positive unbalances as read from the drift plots. Therefore, $a+g(U)m_{SRA}$ in this case is a negative torque and should be corrected with positive torque.

Tumbling tests of gyro units

From the previous discussion on servo runs, it can be seen that the individual unbalance components may be obtained from a set of three servo runs, one IA vertical run, one IA horizontal run and one IA ‖ PA run. However, this is a time-consuming procedure, since at least one complete revolution must be obtained in each position.

The tumbling tests were therefore developed partly to permit measurement of the gyro unbalance components by one test and in as short a time as possible. For example, if the gyro unit is mounted on the turntable with its output axis parallel to the axis of rotation of the turn-table and also parallel to the earth's polar axis, the turntable may be rotated at a high rate (say 10 times earth's rate) with essentially zero-rate input to the gyro unit about the input axis. In this orientation, there is no earth-rate input, since IA travels in a plane perpendicular to the earth's polar axis. The signal-generator output signal is amplified and applied as a correction to the gyro torque generator in order to keep the gyro float at its zero-angle position and thus at the signal-generator null. This is a rate-feedback loop. Given the sensitivity of the torque generator, a record of its input current gives the unbalance of the gyro float about the output axis as a function of the angle of the turntable with respect to a given reference orientation.

The purpose of Derivation Summary 7-5 is to derive a set of un-balance equations for the tumbling test. As before, the unbalance equations are derived with the assumption that positive mass unbalances exist. The standard mounting orientation for tumbling tests is with the gyro-unit output axis aligned parallel to the axis of rotation of the turn-table and also parallel to the earth's polar axis. In this orientation, since the input axis travels in a plane perpendicular to the earth's polar axis and the turntable axis, tumbling tests may be taken either with the wheel rotating or with the wheel stationary, with the turntable rotating clockwise or counterclockwise, and with the turntable rotating at any given rate.

During the tumbling test, if a record is made of the current input to the torque generator, this current will be proportional to the correction torque that is necessary to keep the gyro float at null or, with a change of algebraic sign, proportional to the gyro unbalance. This control current, i_c, flows through one winding of the torque generator; the current flowing through the other winding of the torque generator is fixed for any given test and is called the reference current, $i_{(ref)}$. If the sensitivity of the torque generator, $S_{(tg)\,(i^2,\,W)}$, is known in meru/ma², or dyne-cm/ma², then at any given turntable angle reading the gimbal-rate uncertainty or drift rate is

$$(U)W_g = i_c \cdot i_{(ref)} S_{(tg)\,(i^2,\,W)}$$

A. <u>Tumbling tests about OA</u>. At the start of the run, IA is pointing west in alignment with the zero reference orientation of the turntable.

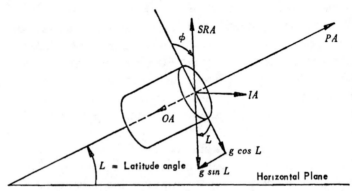

Fig. 7-18. Gyro unit oriented with OA||PA – South.

1. OA||PA – South:

   $(U)M_R$ is a positive torque

   $g(U)m_{(IA)} \cos L \cos \phi$ is a positive torque

   $g(U)m_{(SRA)} \cos L \sin \phi$ is a positive torque

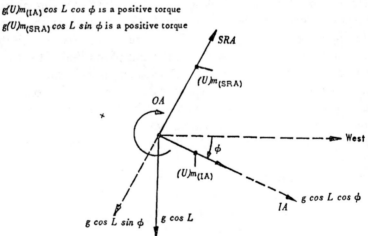

Fig. 7-19. View along OA looking South.

$\frac{1}{k_{(IA)}}$ $mg \cos L \sin \phi$ is a displacement along + IA

Derivation Summary 7-5. Tumbling tests. (Page 1 of 3)

$\frac{1}{k_{(SRA)}}$ $mg \cos L \cos \phi$ is a displacement along $-$SRA

$\frac{1}{k_{(IA)}}$ $m^2 g^2 \cos^2 L \sin \phi \cos \phi$ produces a positive torque

$\frac{1}{k_{(SRA)}}$ $m^2 g^2 \cos^2 L \sin \phi \cos \phi$ produces a negative torque

$$U)M = +(U)M_R + g(U)m_{(SRA)} \cos L \sin \phi + g(U)m_{(IA)} \cos L \cos \phi$$

$$- \left\{ \left[\frac{\frac{1}{k_{(SRA)}} - \frac{1}{k_{(IA)}}}{2} \right] m^2 g^2 \cos^2 L \right\} \sin 2\phi \qquad (1)$$

2. OA$\|$PA $-$ North:

$$U)M = +(U)M_R + g(U)m_{(SRA)} \cos L \sin \phi - g(U)m_{(IA)} \cos L \cos \phi$$

$$+ \left\{ \left[\frac{\frac{1}{k_{(SRA)}} - \frac{1}{k_{(IA)}}}{2} \right] m^2 g^2 \cos^2 L \right\} \sin 2\phi \qquad (2)$$

. Tumbling tests about SRA. At the start of the run, OA is pointing west in alignment with the zero reference orientation of the turntable.

. SRA$\|$PA $-$ South:

$$U)M = +(U)M_R - g(U)m_{(IA)} \sin L - \left\{ \left[\frac{\frac{1}{k_{(SRA)}} - \frac{1}{k_{(IA)}}}{2} \right] m^2 g^2 \sin 2L + g(U)m_{(SRA)} \cos L \right\} \cos \phi \qquad (3)$$

. SRA$\|$PA $-$ North:

$$U)M = +(U)M_R + g(U)m_{(IA)} \sin L - \left\{ \left[\frac{\frac{1}{k_{(SRA)}} - \frac{1}{k_{(IA)}}}{2} \right] m^2 g^2 \sin 2L - g(U)m_{(SRA)} \cos L \right\} \cos \phi \qquad (4)$$

A single tumbling test in this position is not particularly useful in terms of measuring unbalance components, since $g(U)m_{(SRA)}$ cannot be separated from the unbalance due to compliance and $g(U)m_{(IA)}$ cannot be separated from the constant term. This test can be made with the gyro wheel stationary or rotating. The unit is said to be rotated about its sterile axis.

. Tumbling tests about IA. At the start of the run, OA is pointing west in alignment with the zero reference on the turntable. If the gyro wheel is rotating, the turntable must be driven at sidereal rate in the defined clockwise direction to cancel earth's rate. The sidereal time drive must be precise enough, in terms of the uncertainties in the gyro to be tested, so that input rates due to gear-tooth errors may be neglected.

Derivation Summary 7-5. Tumbling tests. (Page 2 of 3)

1. IA $\|$ PA — South:

$$(U)M = +(U)M_R + g(U)m_{(SRA)} \sin L + \left\{ \left[\frac{\frac{1}{k_{(SRA)}} - \frac{1}{k_{(IA)}}}{2} \right] m^2 g^2 \sin 2L - g(U)m_{(IA)} \cos L \right\} \cos \phi \tag{5}$$

2. IA$\|$PA — North:

$$(U)M = +(U)M_R - g(U)m_{(SRA)} \sin L + \left\{ \left[\frac{\frac{1}{k_{(SRA)}} - \frac{1}{k_{(IA)}}}{2} \right] m^2 g^2 \sin 2L + g(U)m_{(IA)} \cos L \right\} \cos \phi \tag{6}$$

None of these tests gives an actual measurement of the magnitude of $k_{(SRA)}$ or $k_{(IA)}$. Only their difference is measured. Thus, determination of the weaker axis for any given gyro can be easily made, but the design of the isoelastic gyro (where $k_{(SRA)} = k_{(IA)}$ and the compliance torque is zero for all orientations)may be much more difficult.

By adjusting the balance nuts on the float, the torques due to $g(U)m_{(IA)}$ and $g(U)m_{(SRA)}$ may be reduced within any given limit. However, since the balance nut itself may not be adequately balanced about its own rotational axis, any rotation of the SRA nut results in a change in the IA unbalance and the unbalance is cross-coupled. This necessitates a series of small adjustments that converge toward zero mass-unbalance.

Derivation Summary 7-5. Tumbling tests. (Page 3 of 3)

If the drift rate is calculated in meru for each ten-degree interval of turntable rotation, a set of 36 readings for each revolution of the turntable is obtained and the data will be similar to the type obtained from the servo runs.

Fourier analysis of test data

The unbalance components for any given revolution of the turntable, either during a servo run or a tumbling test, are obtained by Fourier analysis of the turntable orientation (see Derivation Summary 7-6).

Note that while the tumbling test data give an instantaneous value of rate (calculated from torque), which is read at each ten-degree interval, the servo run data give an *average* value of rate over one ten-degree interval. Therefore, in order to keep the servo run data in phase with the tumbling test data, the elapsed-time recorder on servo runs is actually tripped at 5°, 15°, 25°, etc.

The Fourier analysis may be done on a digital computer that is programmed to give not only the unbalance coefficients but also the residual unbalance as a function of ø after the five unbalance coefficients have been removed. Also computed are the root-mean-square value and the average value of the residual unbalance, the deviation between any two successive runs as a function of ø, the root-mean-square value and the average value of the deviation between any two successive runs, the deviation as a function of ø between a clockwise tumbling test and a counterclockwise tumbling test, and the root-mean-square value and average value of the deviation between a clockwise and a counterclockwise tumbling test. The desired variables (i.e., deviations) are plotted as a function of turntable angle from the digital computer's punched cards by an automatic plotting machine.

The unbalance components for any given revolution of the turntable, either during a servo run or a tumbling test, are obtained by Fourier analysis of the thirty-six pieces of data from one complete revolution of the turntable. Define

$F(\phi) \equiv U(\phi)$ = unbalance as a function of turntable rotation angle, ϕ

Expand this in the trigonometric series

$$F(\phi) = C_0 + C_1 \sin \phi + C_2 \cos \phi + C_3 \sin 2\phi + C_4 \cos 2\phi$$

It can be shown by straightforward Fourier analysis procedures that, if $F(\phi)$ has a power spectrum in which certain high harmonics can be ignored,

$$C_0 = \frac{1}{2\pi} \int_0^{2\pi} F(\phi)\, d\phi = \frac{1}{2\pi} [\text{sum of 36 ordinates}] \frac{2\pi}{36} = \frac{1}{36} \sum_{0^\circ}^{350^\circ} F(\phi)$$

$$C_1 = \frac{1}{\pi} \int_0^{2\pi} F(\phi) \sin \phi \, d\phi = \frac{1}{18} \sum_{0^\circ}^{350^\circ} [F(\phi) \cos \phi]$$

$$C_2 = \frac{1}{\pi} \int_0^{2\pi} F(\phi) \cos \phi \, d\phi = \frac{1}{18} \sum_{0^\circ}^{350^\circ} [F(\phi) \cos \phi]$$

$$C_3 = \frac{1}{\pi} \int_0^{2\pi} F(\phi) \sin 2\phi \, d\phi = \frac{1}{18} \sum_{0^\circ}^{350^\circ} [F(\phi) \sin 2\phi]$$

$$C_4 = \frac{1}{\pi} \int_0^{2\pi} F(\phi) \cos 2\phi \, d\phi = \frac{1}{18} \sum_{0^\circ}^{350^\circ} [F(\phi) \cos 2\phi]$$

Derivation Summary 7-6. Fourier analysis of test data.

CHAPTER 8

APPLICATIONS OF INERTIAL TECHNIQUES

INERTIAL components — gyros, accelerometers, gimbals, and computers are extensible to that broad class of research problems in which instrumented coordinate axes are needed and in which specific force measurement plays a role. A list, by no means exhaustive, would include problems of a geophysical nature, such as are encountered in the fields of oceanography, meteorology and gravimetry; and astronomical problems, such as the making of planetary or stellar measurements from an airborne or satellite-borne observatory. A survey of these applications is presented in what follows.

The application of inertial techniques to oceanography is in the navigational refinement the techniques offer: measurements on the ocean, such as currents and current gradients, the slope of the sea face relative to the direction of gravity, and temperature as a function of depth, all may be more readily located on an earth-grid by inertial techniques than was heretofore possible. Here it should be noted that the inertial methods are dynamic in character; the latitude, longitude, and azimuth reference of a craft are available 'on the run', so to speak. Many measurements which heretofore were static, discrete and discontinuous may now be changed into dynamic continuous-record types of measurement. This proposition applies in a general way to all inertial research applications.

In the field of meterology, measurement techniques frequently parallel oceanographic methods and, therefore, inertial techniques may be expected to find application here also. The effects of upper atmosphere winds and wind gradients on inertial equipment in balloons would be an example of a dynamic inertial measurement in this realm.

Gravimetry represents a special case of the kind of specific force measurement involved in ordinary inertial guidance. However, to determine the shape of the earth's gravity field from, say, an airplane, is to invert the navigation problem; for in navigation, briefly, the field is given, and the geometry must be determined; in gravimetry, the geom-

Fig. 8-1. A typical inertial guidance system installed in an airplane.

etry must be given with high precision, to determine the field. To the extent that gyros can aid in providing a suitable coordinate frame for the specific force measurement, inertial techniques can be of help in establishing the geometry. Recourse is still had to a gravimeter, as the vertical accelerometer in this problem.

In astronomy, one of the persistent problems has always been the interference which the varying index of refraction of the atmosphere presents to good 'seeing'. The overcoming of this difficulty by elevating a telescope in a balloon has been suggested in recent years by the availability of inertial techniques. Thus, star scintillation may be recorded as a function of time at various altitudes by gimballing an automatic star-tracking telescope in a balloon gondola. The balloon, in fact, need have no man in it, if gyros attached to the telescope can be commanded, by telemetry from the ground, to acquire the desired celestial body for the telescope.

All of these applications have the effect of extending the use not only of inertial-guidance components, but also of inertial-guidance design techniques themselves, far beyond the field of navigation. As can be surmised from this book, the design techniques themselves are in part new, and therefore their extension to other fields of effort promises a greater rate of progress in those fields. It is this advance in *instrumentation*, in itself a branch of engineering, that is perhaps one of the largest contributions that the development of inertial guidance will make to the advancement of technology.

In navigation itself, the always-available, interference-proof aspects of inertial guidance will be more widely applied as there are developed smaller, lighter and, particularly, lower-cost equipment without sacrifice of performance ability. Of special interest here is a system that will be economically feasible for transcontinental and transoceanic commercial aircraft.

An actual installation of a typical inertial guidance system in an aircraft is pictured in Fig. 8-1. The system shown was flown from Boston to Los Angeles as a demonstration of the capabilities of an operating system. Films made during the flight were later publicly televised.

The military uses of inertial guidance for submarines, aircraft and missiles are obvious. The use of inertial guidance in new and rapidly growing fields of satellite and interplanetary systems, particularly when coupled with stellar and microwave radiation guidance equipment, offers the next challenge to designers and users of guidance systems.

BIBLIOGRAPHY

1. DRAPER, C. S., 'Flight Control' (The 43rd Wilbur Wright Memorial Lecture), *J. Roy. Aeron. Soc.*, 59, 451-477, July, 1955.

2. BICKNELL, JOSEPH, LARRABEE, E. E., SEAMANS, R. C., JR., and WHITAKER, H. P., 'Automatic Control of Aircraft' (paper presented at Journees Internationales de Sciences Aeronautiques, Paris, France, May, 1957), published by the Instrumentation Laboratory, Massachusetts Institute of Technology, Cambridge, Massachusetts, May, 1957.

3. SCHULER, MAX, 'Die Storung von Pendul — und Kreiselapparaten durch die Beschleunigung der Fahrzeuges', *Physik. Z.*, 24, 1923.

4. WRIGLEY, WALTER, 'Schuler Tuning Characteristics in Navigational Instruments', *Navigation, Journal of the Institute of Navigation*, 2, (No. 8), December, 1950.

5. RAWLINGS, A. L., *The Theory of the Gyroscopic Compass and its Deviations* (2nd ed.), Macmillan, New York, 1944.

6. WRIGLEY, WALTER, 'An Investigation of Methods Available for Indicating the Direction of the Vertical from Moving Bases', ScD. Thesis, Massachusetts Institute of Technology, Cambridge, Massachusetts, 1941.

7. STEWART, C. J., *Aircraft Instruments*, John Wiley, New York, 1930.

8. KOOY, J. M. and UYTENBOGAART, J. W. H., *Ballistics of the Future*, McGraw-Hill, New York, 1946.

9. RUSSELL, W. T., 'Inertial Guidance for Rocket-Propelled Missiles', *Jet Propulsion* (American Rocket Society) (28) 1958.

10. KLASS, PHILIP J., *Inertial Navigation; out of the Laboratory and into Missile Systems*, Aviation Week Special Report, McGraw-Hill, New York, 1956.

11. BARTELS, J. (Editor), *Handbuch der Physik*, Springer Verlag, 1957 (48), p. 542.

12. WRIGLEY, W., WOODBURY, R. B. and HOVORKA, J., *Inertial Guidance*, S.M.F. Fund Paper No. FF-16, Institute of the Aeronautical Sciences, New York, 1957.

13. BARTELS, J. (Editor), *Handbuch der Physik*, Springer Verlag, 1957 (47), p. 223.

14. MITCHELL, H. C., *Definitions of Terms Used in Geodetic and Other Surveys*, Spec. Pub. 242, U.S. Department of Commerce, Coast and Geodetic Survey, 1948.

15. JEFFREYS, HAROLD, *The Earth*, Cambridge University Press, 1952 (new edition).

16. BARTELS, J. (Editor), *Handbuch der Physik*, Springer Verlag, 1957 (47), p. 219.

17. WRIGLEY, W. and HOVORKA, J., 'Orientation Measurements with Gyros and Vertical Indicating Systems', in *Dynamic Measurement* (Edited by Y. T. LI), Department of Aeronautical Engineering, Massachusetts Institute of Technology, Cambridge, Mass., 1956.

18. DRAPER, C. S., McKAY, WALTER and LEES, SIDNEY, *Instrument Engineering*, McGraw-Hill, New York:
    Vol. I   *Methods for Describing the Situations of Instrument Engineering*, 1952.
    Vol. II   *Methods for Associating Mathematical Solutions with Common Forms*, 1953.
    Vol. III   *Application of the Instrument Engineering Method*
               Part 1 *Measurement Systems*, 1955
               Part 2 *Control Systems* (in preparation).

19. HOAG, D. G., *Suggested Specifications for the BuOrd Standard Integrating Gyro 201G*, Report R-91, Instrumentation Laboratory, Massachusetts Institute of Technology, Cambridge, Mass., December, 1955.

20. DRAPER, C. S., WRIGLEY, W. and GROHE, L. R., 'The Floating Integrating Gyro and Its Application to Geometrical Stabilization Problems on Moving Bases', S.M.F. Fund Paper No. FF-13, Institute of the Aeronautical Sciences, New York, 1955.

21. DRAPER, C. S., 'Gyroscopic Apparatus', Application Date: August 2, 1951, U.S. Patent 2,752,790.

22. JAROSH, J. J., HASKELL, C. A. and DUNNELL, W. W., JR., 'Gyroscopic Apparatus', Application Date: February 9, 1951, U.S. Patent 2,752,791.

23. WHITMAN, H. R., WALES, R. L. and ANDERSON, J. P., *The Type H Gyro, Computing and Accelerometer Units*, Report R-17, Instrumentation Laboratory, Massachusetts Institute of Technology, Cambridge 39, Mass., 1953.

24. HOVORKA, J., HURSH, J. W., FREY, E. J., DENHARD, W. G., GROHE, L. R., GILINSON, P. J., JR. and VANDER VELDE, W. E., 'Recent Progress in Inertial Guidance', *American Rocket Society Journal* (29), 1959.

25. GILINSON, P. J., JR., 'The 8-Pole Microsyn Magnetic Suspension Signal and Torque Generator', Engineering Note E-590, Instrumentation Laboratory, Massachusetts Institute of Technology, Cambridge, Mass., October, 1956.

26. GILINSON, P. J., JR., OBERBECK, G. A. and GARCIA, G. C., 'Optimum Operating Point for 8-Pole Microsyn Magnetic Suspension', Engineering Note E-954, Instrumentation Laboratory, Massachusetts Institute of Technology, Cambridge, Mass., November, 1956.

27. GILINSON, P. J., JR., FRAZIER, R. H. and DENHARD, W. G., 'A Magnetic Bearing for Floated Inertial Instruments' (to be published in the Proceedings of the National Specialists Meeting on the Guidance of Aero-Space Vehicles, Institute of the Aeronautical Sciences, Boston, May, 1960).

28. GIANOUKOS, W. A. and PALMER, P. J., *Gyro Test Laboratory Unbalance Equations*, Report GT-130, Instrumentation Laboratory, Massachusetts Institute of Technology, Cambridge, Mass., August, 1957.

SUBJECT INDEX

NAME INDEX

(See also Bibliography, p. 126.)

CPSIA information can be obtained at www.ICGtesting.com
Printed in the USA
BVOW03s0754281114

377069BV00035B/1100/P